PREACHING HARD TEXTS of the OLD TESTAMENT

PREACHING HARD TEXTS of the OLD TESTAMENT

ELIZABETH ACHTEMEIER

HENDRICKSON
PUBLISHERS

© 1998 by Hendrickson Publishers, Inc.
P. O. Box 3473
Peabody, Massachusetts 01961–3473
All rights reserved
Printed in the United States of America

ISBN 1–56563–333–4

Second Printing — April 2000

Library of Congress Cataloging-in-Publication Data

Achtemeier, Elizabeth Rice, 1926–
    Preaching hard texts of the Old Testament   /
Elizabeth Achtemeier.
        Includes bibliographical references and index.
        ISBN 1–56563–333–4 (pbk.)
        1. Bible.   O.T.—Homiletical use.   I. Title.
    BS1191.5.A245   1998
    251—dc21   98–20141
                                                          CIP

The cover art is taken from a painting by Andrea Mantegna (1431–1506); *The Sacrifice of Abraham,* c. 1490; Kunsthistorisches Museum, Vienna, Austria. Photo credit: Erich Lessing/Art Resource, New York, New York.

For our children, who honor the Scriptures

Marie and Paul
Mark and Katherine

Table of Contents

Writings

Prophets and Lamentations

Introduction

Some of the hard texts are hard because they are difficult to understand, others are hard because they represent points of view at odds with our conventional wisdom or with other parts of Scriptures, and still others are hard because they demand too much of us.

Peter Gomes, *The Good Book*[1]

I HAVE ALWAYS THOUGHT, AND IN FACT TAUGHT, THAT IF WE have some problem with a passage in the Old Testament, it is not the Bible's problem. It is ours. The Old Testament has been handed down to us in the church as a priceless treasure. In it, our Israelite forebears in the faith have preserved for us some eighteen hundred years of their witness to what the one God has said and done in their lives. Through their faithful testimony, the Holy One of Israel who is at the same time the God and Father of our Lord Jesus Christ has revealed himself. Through the words of his historians and prophets, psalmists and wisdom teachers, priests and lawgivers, God has formed our faith, instructed our piety in proper reverence and awe, awakened our expectations of his working, and bent our wills to his desires and goals. Apart from the Old Testament, we do not know who the Father of Jesus Christ is nor do we know who we are as "the Israel of God" (Gal 6:16).[2]

So we have to preach from the Old Testament. For some preachers, constructing a sermon from any portion of this two-thirds of our canon is a problem, because they have not read and studied the Old Testament and therefore do not know it. They approach it with all of the usual stereotypes—that the Old Testament is a legalistic book, that its God is not a loving Father but only a God of wrath, that its theology and worship are primitive and outdated, that its truths have been superseded by the "higher spiritual truths" of the New Testament. None of these stereotypes is valid, and those who preach them are not preaching the gospel.

Such ignorant assessments of the Old Testament are not our principle concern in this book, however. Rather, even for those of us who preach regularly from the Old Testament and who could not do without it, as the church for two thousand years has said it cannot do without it, there are passages in the Old Testament that give us trouble.

Barbara Taylor wrote a wonderful article some years ago about her experience of being asked to address a senior citizens' group on "Women in the Old Testament." She told them the stories about Jael who drove a tent peg through Sisera's temple and about Esther who won permission for the Jews to destroy seventy-five thousand of their enemies. "They thanked me very much," Taylor said, "and have never asked me back."[3]

Such stories and many others in the Old Testament do not fit with our views of God. This is where the difficulty arises. God does things and says things in the Old Testament accounts that we do not like, just as Jesus does and says similarly unsavory things in the New Testament.[4] We preachers too, for all of our knowledge of the Scriptures, have stereotypes of God, and if his deeds and words do not match those preformed views, we reject or ignore them. We are very good at excising or omitting passages in the Old Testament that we cannot countenance. We form a "canon within the canon" and preach only that with which we agree.

As stated above, however, the difficulties that we encounter with parts of the Old Testament are not the Old

Testament's problems. They are ours. We are required to wrestle with these difficult texts until we can come to some peace with them. We are not to bring our views of God to the texts; rather, we are to attempt to let the texts shape our views of God and his working. As Karl Barth wrote,

> The gospel is not in our thoughts or hearts; it is in Scripture. The dearest habits and best insights that I have—I must give them all up before listening. I must not use them to protect myself against the breakthrough of a knowledge that derives from Scripture. Again and again I must let myself be contradicted. I must let myself be loosened up. I must be able to surrender everything.[5]

This book, therefore, is an attempt at wrestling, at surrendering, at letting some of the difficult passages of the Old Testament have their way with us preachers.

Obviously, this little volume cannot treat all of the texts over which faithful preachers stumble. Every preacher has his or her own list. Rather it deals only with selected texts from which preachers might possibly write sermons. Please keep this in mind if a text is omitted that you feel should have been dealt with. My husband facetiously recommended that I deal with the brief story in 2 Kgs 2:23–24 of the two she-bears mauling the little boys who made fun of the prophet Elisha. While the story is a folktale reflecting the popular fear of prophetic men of God, I pointed out that no one was going to preach on it, not even to stand up for bald-headed men!

Some effort has been made to take account of the three-year common lectionary[6] and to deal with those stated Old Testament texts that might possibly give preachers difficulty. But many nonlectionary texts are treated as well. Even a three-year lectionary can specify only a limited number of Old Testament passages, and there are many others that have been largely ignored but that should be preached if the congregation is to hear "the whole counsel of God."

The exposition of some texts in this work can be applied to other Old Testament passages. For example, the chapter on "The LORD Is a Man of War" from Exod 15 contains some thoughts about God's destruction of his enemies that can

apply to similar militaristic texts. Likewise, the treatment of
Jeremiah's prophetic action in Jer 13 contains a discussion
that applies to most prophetic symbolic actions. The exposition of God's use of natural catastrophes (Amos 4:4–13) may
throw some light on other texts dealing with God's use of the
natural world. And much of the treatment of the Day of the
Lord in Zeph 1:14–18 applies to other texts dealing with that
fateful day.

I omit discussions of some passages because I do not
want to repeat what I have written in other books. For example, I have a full treatment of the Book of Jonah and of Hos
2:14–23 in my volume *Minor Prophets I,*[7] just as I fully expound
Gen 3:1–24 in *Preaching Biblical Texts.*[8] In similar vein, the
Book of Zechariah is full of preachable texts, especially in its
vision sections, but I have dealt with these in my commentary
Nahum–Malachi[9] in the Interpretation commentary series.
There are some repeated discussions in this book, however,
of the Holy War and the holiness of God made necessary by
the treatment of individual texts.

The translation of the Old Testament used is that of the
Revised Standard Version unless otherwise noted. While the
marketeers have striven mightily to replace the widely-used
RSV with the New Revised Standard Version, and while that
latter properly uses inclusive language for human beings, many
scholars have found fault with the NRSV in its rendering of the
original Hebrew. Similarly, after having written a commentary
employing the New International Version (NIV)[10] that is so
widely used among conservatives, I have concluded that probably the RSV is still the most faithful—and most beautiful—
rendering of the original Hebrew of the Old Testament.

Notes

1. *Reading the Bible with Mind and Heart* (New York: Morrow, 1996), 74.

2. For a full discussion, see my book *Preaching from the Old Testament* (Louisville: Westminster/John Knox, 1989).

3. "Preaching the Terrors," *Journal for Preachers* 15 (2, 1992): 3.

4. See *Preaching the Hard Sayings of Jesus* by John T. and James R. Carroll (Peabody, Mass.: Hendrickson, 1996). After publishing that volume, Hendrickson Publishers asked me to write this one about the Old Testament.

5. Karl Barth, *Homiletics* (trans. Geoffrey W. Bromiley and Donald E. Daniels; Louisville: Westminster/John Knox, 1991), 78.

6. The three-year revised common lectionary is the list of biblical texts that have been designated for each Sunday of the church year by the ecumenical Consultation on Common Texts. It includes both Old and New Testament texts to be used over a period of three years. It is used by many churches, especially those that have a more liturgical service.

7. New International Biblical Commentary. Peabody, Mass.: Hendrickson, 1996.

8. *Preaching Biblical Texts: Expositions by Jewish and Christian Scholars* (ed. Fredrick C. Holmgren and Herman E. Schaalman; Grand Rapids: Eerdmans, 1995), 1–10.

9. Interpretation: A Bible Commentary for Teaching and Preaching; Atlanta: John Knox, 1986.

10. *Minor Prophets I.*

❧ 1 ❧

The Holy One of Israel

I WAS ONCE ASKED IN AN INTERVIEW TO EXPLAIN SOME OF the characteristics that separate great preaching from mediocre preaching. Without going into all of the details of my response, probably the principle thing that should be said is that great preachers talk mostly about God and not about human problems. It is very easy for anybody to tell what is wrong with our world and what are the common struggles and sins of us human beings. We have only to look about us or to read the morning headlines. Even a twelve year old can compile of list of the evils in our society. But it takes a preacher to say what God is doing about them.

Great preaching talks mostly about God. In order to set the following discussions of specific difficult passages in their context, perhaps we need to say some things about God—about this Holy One of Israel, this Mighty One of Jacob, this Redeemer and Rock and Fortress and Father of his chosen people—before we move into specific problems.

Through the proclamations of Second Isaiah, we hear the following:

> . . . my thoughts are not your thoughts,
>   neither are your ways my ways, says the LORD.
> For as the heavens are higher than the earth,
>   so are my ways higher than your ways,
>   and my thoughts than your thoughts. (Isa 55:8–9)

Thus we are warned to eschew every attempt to put God in the boxes of our prior stereotypes. We all have views of who and what the God of the Bible should be like. But "to whom then will you compare me, that I should be like him? says the Holy One" (Isa 40:25). The God of the Bible comes to us as the Holy One, as the One who is totally other than anything or anyone in all creation. We cannot encompass his thoughts or capture his person in a comparison, nor can we predict his ways. Where we think justice should be meted out, we are surprised by incredible mercy. Where we believe surely there is reason for forgiveness, stern wrath is spoken instead. Our definitions of power become weakness, and our weaknesses are shown to be strength. Our estimates of wisdom are exposed as nothing but foolishness, while the foolishness of God's actions becomes the only truth.

This God of the Old Testament—and of the New—does not conform to our expectations or consider himself bound by our pious definitions. In everything and all, he remains the Lord. And so we cannot judge the biblical witness to God or discard any part of it as unworthy of deity. We can only listen to the words of witness and learn of this incomparable Holy One.

Several things are certain, however. Everywhere throughout the biblical witness, the God of Israel wills life. The world he makes is a planet simply teeming with life. Every drop of pond water is filled with hundreds of microbes, every sky populated with a million birds. Roots thrust out until they burst through rock, and plants blossom out of dry ground. Creatures of every shape and form inhabit jungle and plain, bush and desert. Despite all its thorns and thistles, the earth gives its produce. The work of the Creator brings forth unimaginable life.

If we cannot read God's will for life from the creation around us, then perhaps we can hear it from the biblical word. "I have no pleasure in the death of any one," says the Lord God (Ezek 18:32). And so when killing and violence that come from our sin devastate human life, the Old Testament tells us that it grieves God "to his heart" (Gen 6:6). His plans

2

for our future envision a realm in which "the wolf shall dwell
with the lamb" (Isa 11:6) and "nations shall beat their swords
into plowshares" (Isa 2:4), in which "they shall sit every man
under his vine and under his fig tree, and none shall make
them afraid" (Mic 4:4).

> Steadfast love and faithfulness will meet;
>   righteousness and peace will kiss each other.
> Faithfulness will spring up from the ground,
>   and righteousness will look down from the sky.
>   (Ps 85:10–11)

Are those not the plans of God that we should remember
when we read some difficult passage in the Bible? This Holy
One of Israel wills that we have life. He works with us and
with his creation to restore the fullness of life to all, that
fullness that God created and that he intended from the
beginning.

This God stands opposed, however, to all who would
disrupt his plans, to all those who by human power would en-
slave or oppress the lives he has given, to all who would bend
his just will and ignore his equity and make light of his
righteous, lordly rule. The God of the Bible is a jealous God,
a zealous God,[1] pressing on toward his good goal for his world.
And he will not countenance the evil with which human
beings want to distort and disrupt. God is "of purer eyes than
to behold evil," proclaims Habakkuk, and he "cannot look on
wrong" (Hab 1:13). The Psalmist echoes that:

> The eyes of the LORD are toward the righteous,
>   and his ears toward their cry.
> The face of the LORD is against evildoers,
>   to cut off the remembrance of them from
>   the earth. (Ps 34:15–16)

So it is that in Old Testament, and New, God destroys the
wicked: fire and brimstone rain down on Sodom; the troops
of an oppressing Pharaoh are drowned in the sea; proud
nations are plucked up and wither; false prophets are slain.
Even a faithless northern Israel goes into exile and disappears
from history, and corrupted Judah loses her nationhood and

languishes in Babylonian exile. The Lord, in Jeremiah, puts it in awful terms:

> My heritage has become to me
>> like a lion in the forest,
> she has lifted up her voice against me;
>> therefore I hate her. (Jer 12:8)

The God of the Bible is a hater of evil.

We quail before such a witness, of course, because it turns upside down the assurance of Paul: "If God is for us, who is against us" (Rom 8:31). The awful reverse is, "If God is against us, who can be for us?" And the answer is, "No one." That God can hate anyone goes against everything we have heard of him, and we soften the thought until God never despises anyone, nor does he ever bring any sort of judgment or wrath upon them. God only loves and forgives. Such is our modern conception of him.

Thus we become very much like Israel in the time of Hosea, when it reassured itself that God would always forgive it. Hosea quotes his people's careless words:

> Come, let us return to the LORD;
>> for he has torn, that he may heal us;
>> he has stricken, and he will bind us up.
> After two days he will revive us;
>> on the third day he will raise us up,
>> that we may live before him.
> Let us know, let us press on to know the LORD;
>> his going forth is sure as the dawn;
> he will come to us as the showers,
>> as the spring rains that water the earth. (Hos 6:1–3)

In similar fashion, Judah in Jeremiah's time thought it could do anything and yet be saved. Jeremiah, in his famous Temple Sermon that is quoted by Jesus (Mark 11:17 and parallels), told Judah otherwise:

> Will you steal, murder, commit adultery, swear falsely, burn incense to Ba'al, and go after other gods that you have not known, and then come and stand before me in this house, which is called by my name, and say, "We are delivered!"—only

to go on doing all these abominations? Has this house, which is called by my name become a den of robbers [i.e., a hiding place] in your eyes? (Jer 7:9–11)

In the second century A.D., a man named Marcion thought that God only loved. He declared that the God of the Old Testament was not the God of the New. The Old Testament, with its judging God, was to be discarded, he said. Only the Gospel according to Luke and the ten letters of Paul were to be kept. God was wholly a good God, who never judged anyone.

Tertullian, a writer of the early third century replied to Marcion:

> What a prevaricator of truth is such a god! What a dissembler with his own decision! Afraid to condemn what he really condemns, afraid to hate what he does not love, permitting that to be done which he does not allow, choosing to indicate what he dislikes rather than deeply examine it! This will turn out an imaginary goodness.[2]

The true God is not otherwise fully good than as an enemy of evil, and the Bible from beginning to end declares that of him. Some of the passages that we stumble over in the Old Testament portray God as that enemy. And perhaps we shall never understand the judgment on us by the cross of Christ until we absorb that witness.

But how patient is this Holy One of Israel with our foolishness and follies! He is "very slow to anger," proclaims the prophet Nahum (1:3), and how true that is in the biblical record! Indeed, the description of God as "slow to anger and abounding in steadfast love" is unfailingly found in Israel's ancient creed (Exod 34:6; Num 14:18; Neh 9:17; Ps 86:15; 103:8; 145:8; Joel 2:13; Jonah 4:2). God "remembers that we are dust" (Ps 103:14) and pities our helpless condition (cf. Amos 7:2, 5), and so time and again he withholds his judgment. He constantly sends saving "judges" to rescue an idolatrous Israel from its enemies. He patiently listens to the pleas of his prophets to spare his guilty people (cf. Exod 32:11–14; Deut 9:18–20, 25–27; Amos 7:3, 6). Time and again he "passes over" sin (cf. Rom 3:25) and uses human evil, despite

5

his hatred of it, to further his good purpose (cf. the story of Joseph or of Solomon's accession to the throne). This God of the Old Testament is very slow to anger.

Perhaps the reason for this slowness to anger is that God wishes for us only good. "Oh that they had such a mind as this always, to fear me and to keep all my commandments," the Lord longingly tells Moses, "that it might go well with them and with their children for ever" (Deut 5:29). This Holy One of the Scriptures wants it to go well with us. He wants for us only good (cf. Mic 6:8a). If we absorb nothing else from the biblical witness, we should hear from hundreds of passages that God is good (e.g., Ps 25:8; 34:8). Thus even his commandments are designed only to do us good, to point us in the direction of life abundant, to give us guidance in the new life God grants instead of letting us wander aimlessly in the wilderness.

Because God is good, his judgments on his chosen folk are not about vengeance for wrong but are about correction that aims toward salvation, and this too we must remember when reading the Old Testament. God cannot give us new life without doing away with the old. Jesus puts that explicitly in the New Testament.

> No one puts a piece of unshrunk cloth on an old garment, for the patch tears away from the garment, and a worse tear is made. Neither is new wine put into old wineskins; if it is, the skins burst, and the wine is spilled, and the skins are destroyed; but new wine is put into fresh wineskins, and so both are preserved. (Matt 9:16–17)

The northern kingdom of Israel is sent into exile to rid it of its idolatrous Baal worship and to give it new gifts of righteousness and faithfulness (Hos 2:16–20). There Israel will dwell many days "without king or prince, without sacrifice or pillar, without ephod or teraphim. Afterward the children of Israel shall return and seek the LORD." (Hos 3:4–5). In the same manner, Judah languishes in Babylonia until God can cleanse her from all her sin and give her a new heart and a new obedient spirit (Ezek 36:25–26), writing his law on her heart and entering into covenant with her once again (Jer 31:31–34).

God works to change his elect into new creatures, using his judgments to do away with the old in order that the new people may be born.

"Behold, the Lamb of God, who takes away the sin of the world," John the Baptist says of Jesus (John 1:29). And it is that "taking away" that governs God's radical, judgmental cleansings of us. We die with Christ in baptism, writes Paul (Rom 6:1–4). The old life, by God's judgments on it, is buried six feet under. But all in order that we may be raised to walk in newness of life.

So it is that the Holy One of Israel is finally the saving God. And that is solely because he is merciful and gracious, loving us with a love that will not let us go, despite the fact that we are undeserving. "How can I give you up, O Ephraim?" he sobs in Hosea 11:8. "How can I hand you over, O Israel?" At the core of the character of the God of the Bible is a persistent love for his children.

> Is Ephraim my dear son?
>   Is he my darling child?
> For as often as I speak against him,
>   I do remember him still.
> Therefore my heart yearns for him;
>   I will surely have mercy on him,
>   says the LORD. (Jer 31:20)

The result is that every prophecy and narrative of judgment in the Old Testament leads finally to a "future and a hope," to "plans for welfare and not for evil" (Jer 29:11). Indeed, the whole Old Testament story concerns God's working to take our cursed and death-filled situation and to turn it all into blessing—such is the import of the beginning of the story in Gen 1–12 (esp. Gen 12:3). That the story finds its fulfillment in our sins borne on a cross and overcome in a resurrection is an ending that is consonant with all that has gone before.

The Old Testament witnesses to the same God to which the New Testament gives testimony. We must remember this when dealing with what we consider to be the Old Testament's hard texts.

7

Notes

1. The root word *qin'ah* is translated both as "jealous" and as "zealous" in the Old Testament. God's jealousy is his zeal, his burning purpose to make his world good again.

2. *Tertullian against Marcion* 1.27, cf. 1.26–27; 2.12 (*Ante-Nicene Fathers;* ed. Alexander Roberts and James Donaldson, 1868; repr., Peabody, Mass.: Hendrickson, 1994), 3:292, cf. 3:291–293; 3:307.

PART ONE

Narratives and Law

❧ 2 ❧

"He Shall Rule over You"

GENESIS 3:14–19

Plumbing the Text

I HAVE LIFTED THIS PASSAGE OUT OF ITS CONTEXT FOR THE purpose of our discussion, and I intend to concentrate only on v. 16. But properly the verse and passage are parts of the whole of Gen 3, and it is that entire chapter that the preacher will want to use as the Scripture reading for the day.

Genesis 2–4; 6–8; 9:18–28; and 11:1–9 form a primeval history of the sin of the human race. They are not intended by their author(s) as the stories of human beginnings, but rather as the portrayal of all persons' rebellion against their Creator God. They picture the spread of that rebellion through all the areas of human life and the deadly effects of that rebellion. "Adam" in the story is the Hebrew name for human-kind, and the history of Adam and his descendants is intended to be the story of all of us in our sinful relation to God. As such, Gen 3–11 forms the universal background of the promise to Abraham in Gen 12:1–3 and the explanation of why it was necessary for God to break into history and to give that promise.

In this Genesis history of us all, there is a repeated pattern of sin that grows ever more widespread, of the divine judgment that grows increasingly severe, and of the covering grace of God that nevertheless tempers God's judgment.

Our verse in Gen 3:16 makes up part of the judgment that God causes to fall upon Eve who, with her husband, has eaten the forbidden fruit in the garden. Adam and Eve were set into a paradise that was "very good" (cf. 1:31). Yet, limitations on their existence were an integral part of that good life. By obeying God's command not to eat of the fruit of the tree of the knowledge of good and evil (v. 17), they would acknowledge that they were not their own masters, but rather that the Lord's will was to be the guide of their lives.

The sin of Adam and Eve is their attempt to escape that limitation, to decide for themselves what is right and wrong, to be their own masters and shapers of their own future, to be their own gods. "You will be like God, knowing good and evil," the serpent tells Eve (Gen 3:5). She and her husband wish to slip the limitations of creaturehood and dependence on the Lord in order to be autonomous, self-ruled, independent selves—a goal that is also highly prized in our day. These are the stories of our lives!

Despite Adam and Eve's attempt to be independent of God, they remain always responsible to him and his commands. God therefore speaks his judgment on the serpent, the woman, and the man in turn (vv. 14–19). Adam and Eve, and all humankind with them, are condemned to the judgment of death (v. 19). They are banished from the garden, and guards are set at the entrance to paradise to prevent their return (v. 24). Only God can remove the guards. By their attempts to make God unnecessary, human beings have passed the point of no return.

The judgment that God levels on the woman is pain in childbearing and humiliating domination by her husband. "He shall rule over you." Here begins that battle of the sexes against which the women's movement in our time has raised an agonized cry.

That such domination of the male over the female was not the Creator God's intention in the beginning is clear from Gen 2. The woman was created by God to be a "helper *kenegdo*," that is, a helper *corresponding to* the man (vv. 18, 20)—one like himself, his mutual partner, with whom he could care and share and commune in equality. Further, the woman was to join flesh with her husband in the joyful oneness of marriage (v. 23–25). Now that oneness is broken (v. 7), his ego stands over and against her ego, and sexual union resulting in childbirth becomes something that threatens the woman's life. Her desire is still for her husband, but he shall now be the ruler over her (v. 16).

Forming the Sermon

Thousands of women have suffered under the judgment of Gen 3:16; indeed, the verse is intended to picture human life as it is in its sinful condition, and it does so. This *is* the story of our lives and of our world! And the history that follows in the Old Testament from Gen 12 on is indeed a history of sin, a history marred repeatedly by Israel's attempt to run its own life rather than to rely on its Creator as the Guide and Sustainer of its existence. Always, like Israel, all human beings try to shake free from dependence on God, and always, like Israel, we find ourselves nevertheless responsible to him and his commandments. Thus always, like Israel, we live under God's judgments on our sinful ways.

Let us put it clearly: As long as we try to make God unnecessary in our lives, as long as we try to be our own gods, as long as we think to be autonomous, self-ruling souls, males will always rule over females. That is the judgment under which supposedly autonomous human beings live. And the rule that males exercise is a rule of power. Not only physically but also psychically, intellectually, historically, sociologically, males claim power over women. Women are said to be the "weaker sex," emotionally unstable, unable to reason dispassionately, not equal to the rough and tumble of the world, always needing to be guarded and helped by their superior men. Such are the stereotypes with which females have been characterized.

The result in our time is that the women's movement seeks power. "Power and How to Get It" was the subject of a university women's forum. Women seek to show that they are physically the equal of men—in the armed forces and military academies. They attempt to prove that they don't need men at all; they are autonomous and self-ruled, they claim, and some even think men are "the enemy." For a radical feminist the only sin of a woman is to be dependent on someone else, whether that be a person or God. The Christian faith, since it calls for such dependence on the Lord, cannot be the religion for these feminists. No, they make their own religion, and they re-imagine their own goddess. "You can be like God, knowing good and evil," claimed the serpent (Gen 3:5), and some radical feminists have set out to prove that such is indeed the case, even approving of Eve's attempt to take charge of her own life.

It cannot be denied that the women's movement has gained some benefits for women. More educational opportunities and occupations are now open to females. Many women have gained a new feeling of self-worth and no longer feel that they have stature only from their husbands' accomplishments. Some marriages have taken on the nature of an equal partnership, rather than that of a male-dominated hierarchy. But there have also been evil consequences from women's push for autonomous power. Some marriages have been destroyed; lesbianism and abortion have been claimed as "rights"; university programs have had to knuckle under to often inferior "women's studies"; males have often found themselves outranked in the job market by less qualified females. As for the church, its worship, its liturgy, its hymns, its Bible have been altered to suit feminist dictates. Women have indeed gained power for themselves, but that has not been an unqualified blessing, and the sinful warfare between females and males seems to be as present as ever. A rebellious world still lives under the judgment of the God who is Lord.

Is there any way in which God's intended unity between female and male has been restored and the judgment has been overturned by grace? After all, the history in the entire Bible tells us that despite God's just judgment on all our sins, his mercy and grace have been triumphant in forgiving us and counting us righteous through the sacrifice of Jesus Christ.

14

"While we were yet sinners, Christ died for us" (Rom 5:8). Out of that justification and redemption have come a new relationship with our God and the possibility of a new and transformed life in his Spirit. Can the same be said with respect to the relations between male and female?

Yes indeed. Because of the cross and resurrection of Jesus Christ, the Apostle Paul tells us that male and female are now one in Christ Jesus (Gal 3:28). The ancient split, caused by our sin, has now been overcome. Male and female have been restored to the joyful unity in God that he intended in the beginning. And the result is that the search for autonomous power is now left behind. No longer does the Christian man or woman attempt to rule over the other. Now both are joined together in a mutual service of God and his will. So Paul can call Phoebe, that leader of the house church at Cenchreae, his equal "helper" in the Lord (Rom 16:1–3). He can greet Prisca (Priscilla) as his "fellow worker" in Christ Jesus (Rom 16:3).

In our day, that means that Christian marriage now can become once again a joyful unity, with power shared between husband and wife. It means that women and men may serve side by side in the church, equally called, equally gifted, equally regarded. It means that the awful battle between the sexes is now stilled, and Christians can regard one another as the persons they really are, redeemed servants of the Lord God, from whom they have all good, all guidance, all life.

The battle between the sexes will undoubtedly continue in our society and throughout our world for years, as it has continued for centuries before. But in the church we know that the battle has been stilled and the love of Christ has joined women and men together. We need to proclaim and live out this message within the church. But we must also take it to all the world.[1]

Notes

1. Questions are frequently raised by biblically oriented Christians about those passages in 1 Cor, 1 and 2 Tim, Titus, and Eph 5

in which Christian women seem to be subordinated to men in the church.

In 1 Cor, Paul thinks it quite proper for women to prophesy in church, as long as they cover their heads, in the manner customary to women in public (1 Cor 11:4–16). This seems to be contradicted by Paul's statement in 1 Cor 14:33b–36 that women should keep silent in the church. It is now the view of many scholars that in vv. 33b–35, Paul is quoting other men ("you" in v. 36 is a masculine plural), and that he refutes their argument with the scorn for their view given in v. 36, reflecting his view of the oneness of male and female in Christ.

First and Second Timothy and Titus, which are recognized by all but conservative scholars to be Pauline pseudepigrapha (written not by the apostle himself but by those who continue in his tradition), are very much local letters, and they give vivid descriptions of the difficulty that some local churches are having with some women (and men) in their congregations (see 1 Tim 1:3–7; 2:9; 5:6, 13–16; 2 Tim 3:1–9; 4:3–4; Titus 2:3–5; 3:9). It is clear that not only are some of the women engaging in scandalous behavior, thus discrediting the gospel, but that some of them, who were forbidden to be educated in the Torah in their homes, were being led astray by Gnostic heretics. It is little wonder therefore that the writers of these letters did not want such women teaching and prophesying in the church. We also would not!

Finally, Eph 5:21–33, again a portion of a letter written in the Pauline tradition, urges upon husband and wife mutual service of one another out of reverence for Christ (v. 21). To be sure, the letter assumes a patriarchal setting, in which the husband is the head of the household. However, that headship is totally transformed by the faith, so that the husband's headship is to consist in the faithfulness, service, and self-sacrifice that Christ extended to the church. The headship is no longer a hierarchical rule! Rather, it is self-giving. When such is the nature of the husband's relation to his wife, their marriage becomes a symbol of Christ's relation to his church.

In the Christian faith, there is no valid support for the subjection of female to male. But it should be noted that such equality is established only through Jesus Christ.

❧ 3 ❧

The Sacrifice of Isaac

GENESIS 22:1–19

*T*HIS IS ONE OF THE MOST FAMOUS STORIES IN THE WORLD. It is a text for Easter Vigil in the three-year common lectionary. Despite the spareness of its language, it possesses an aura of horror and love, of obedience and mystery that has fascinated readers for years. Known as "the binding of Isaac," *akedat yitzchak*, by the Jews and as "the sacrifice of Isaac" by Christians, it has been the subject of countless commentaries and sermons and of multiple works of art. I turned a corner on the Harvard University campus one morning to find myself confronted by a bronze statue of Abraham with his knife raised above Isaac's breast.

No story has given Christian readers of the Old Testament more difficulty, however. One frequently hears some faithful churchgoer say, "That story has always troubled me," and so there have been multiple attempts to soften the narrative in order to make it less objectionable. A common approach is to maintain that Abraham, with his pagan background in Mesopotamia, mistakenly believed that God wanted him to sacrifice his son. Even the great Danish theologian Søren Kierkegaard made up a series of fanciful endings to the story. Abraham killed himself instead of Isaac, imagined Kierkegaard. Or Abraham pretended that his actions were the result of temporary insanity. And the wife of Martin Luther objected. "Martin," she said, "I don't believe God would ask anyone to sacrifice his son."

We can understand all of those objections, but we must see that they all discount or distort the biblical text, and it is that text we are called to preach. Not to do so is to miss some of the profundity of the biblical story.

Plumbing the Text

Perhaps most noticeable in this passage are its repetitions: to catch the flavor of the text, preachers should read it slowly and aloud.

"Here am I." Three times Abraham makes this response (vv. 1, 7, 11), and each time he does it signals a different attitude. Over and over again we read "your son, your only son," "his son," "his son," "my son," "my son," "his son," "your son, your only son," "his son," "your son, your only son." And echoing that is "his father," and "my father." Then comes the repeated phrase, "So they went both of them together." Are any other words necessary to describe the loving relation between Abraham and Isaac?

No emotions are described in this text, but the repetitions are full of feeling. The passage has been ascribed to the Elohist, but whoever was the author, he was a masterful storyteller. Not a word is said about how Abraham feels or about Isaac's response. Father and son go on their three-day journey in the utter silence of love. Abraham himself carries the knife and the fire, lest the boy hurt himself with them— perhaps one more indication of the tenderness involved in the story.

Nothing is said of Sarah and what she thinks about the whole affair. Indeed, after this event, nothing further is recorded of Sarah except her death at Hebron (23:2) and her burial in the field of Machpelah (23:19). Over the whole tale lies a touching reticence, and such restraint on the part of the storyteller should mark also the preacher's sermon. We should not speculate about what the text does not say.

Forming the Sermon

The passage begins, "After these things," and we need to ask, "What things?" Most important, of course, is the fact that Isaac has been born in Abraham and Sarah's old age (Gen 21:1–8), in fulfillment of God's promise that he will give them many descendants (Gen 12:2; 15:5; 17:2–6). God sets out, through Abraham and his offspring, to reverse the cursed effects of our sinful rebellion against him. At the end of Gen 11, human sin has corrupted God's "good" creation (Gen 1:31) so that husband is set against wife (Gen 3), brother against brother (Gen 4), one man against another (Lamech, Gen 4), nation against nation (Gen 11). God's good gifts of beauty and work, marriage and family, fruitfulness and community have been ruined, and over the earth hangs the sentence of death that is the wages of sin. Genesis 1–11 is the story of us all. But in Gen 12:1–3, God tells Abraham that he will use him and his descendants to reverse that story of fallenness and to bring blessing on all the families of the earth. Abraham and his descendants are the bearers of the promise of salvation for humankind.

Abraham, however, is no paragon of faith, nor is Sarah his wife a model believer. Despite the fact that Abraham obeyed God's command to leave his country and home and relatives in Haran in Mesopotamia (Gen 12:4), Abraham did not initially believe God when the Lord told him he would have a son. In Gen 15:1–3, he at first flatly contradicts God's promise to him. In Gen 17:17–18, he falls on his face and laughs when told the promise. Sarah joins in the unbelieving laughter in Gen 18:12–13.

Similarly, Abraham does a lot of questioning of the Lord in the passages preceding the sacrifice of Isaac. In Gen 18:22–33 he asks God if the Lord is a Judge who will do "right" by Sodom. And in Gen 21:11, Abraham is not at all pleased that God orders him to placate Sarah and send away his slave woman Hagar and her son Ishmael, who is Abraham's actual first-born. In short, Abraham and Sarah are spasmodic believers, who do a lot of questioning of God, as we ourselves so often do.

19

The result in our passage is, "God tested Abraham," v. 1 (cf. Heb 11:17). We must not water down that assertion. God's promise of blessing for the world rides on the faith and obedience of Abraham, who has been chosen to be the medium of blessing. And the response that Abraham makes to God's test is absolutely crucial for God's purpose for the world. On what a slender thread God sometimes hangs his plan for this planet! Abraham has been given the gift of Isaac in fulfillment of God's word. Now the question is, Whom does Abraham trust? Does he trust the gift and cling to Isaac? Or does he trust the Giver, God, and believe that God knows what he is doing?

The thought that God tests his servants is a familiar one in the Scriptures. For example, Israel's entrance into the promised land is a testing of her loyalty to the Lord, to see if she will go after the gods of other nations or if she will in fact be the people through whom God can bring his blessing on all (cf. Judg 2:22; 3:1, 4). Her deprivations in the wilderness were a test of her trust in the God who went before and behind her (Deut 8:2, 16; 33:8; Ps 81:7; Heb 3:8). Her defeat by foreigners is a test of her faith in her Refuge and Strength (Ps 66:10).

Similarly, our Lord Jesus is tested by his Father in the Garden of Gethsemane. Jesus tests Philip at the feeding of the five thousand (John 6:6). And James writes, "Count it all joy, my brethren, when you meet various trials, for you know that the testing of your faith produces steadfastness" (Jas 1:2–3; cf. 2 Cor 8:2).

We must not think, however, that God's test of our trust in him is behind every single affliction that we suffer. In the Scriptures, God tests his servants *when his purpose is at stake.* For example, it is of crucial importance in God's plan that Israel remains faithful to him during her wanderings through the wilderness and her residency in the promised land. It is of paramount importance that Jesus Christ determines in Gethsemane to follow God's will and not his own. It is very important that persecuted Christians do not waver in their faith and witness to the world. In our time, we could say that it was absolutely necessary that the Confessing Church stand opposed to Adolph Hitler, just as it is important for every Christian in our secular society never to be "ashamed of the Gospel" (Rom 1:16) despite the scorn and disbelief and immoral lifestyle of those around them. God is working out a purpose in our world, and he does indeed sometimes test us as to the steadfastness of our faith in him, to see whether or not he can use us in his purpose. For that reason, "God tested Abraham" (v. 1).

Abraham, in our passage, passes the test, and so God provides a ram to be sacrificed instead of Isaac, vv. 13–14. The promise is renewed for the father of our faith, vv. 15–18, and God's saving work can proceed according to his initial plan.

Israel always saw her own experience in these ancient stories of the patriarchs, and this story of the binding of Isaac became for her a mirror of the pain she suffered throughout her history, because she was God's chosen people. God's election of us is never without a cost. Far from being a call to privilege, it is frequently a summons to suffer for the sake of our faith, often to bear reproach or marginalization from a secular society, but sometimes also to undergo sacrifice and even crucifixion.

Indeed, anyone who has carefully studied this Genesis text cannot help but be struck by the parallel it forms to the passion of our Lord. It is quite appropriate that it is the stated Old Testament lesson in some lectionaries for the first Sunday in Lent or for the Easter vigil.

Surely, in the story of Jesus we have the picture of a Father and a Son, a Son and Father, going both of them together to Moriah. A later passage in 2 Chron 3:1 even identifies Moriah with Jerusalem. So the Father and his beloved begotten Son go up to Jerusalem together. "My Father and I are one," Jesus said. He makes his last journey in the company of God his Father.

The Son Jesus trusts his Father with his life, just as Isaac trusted Abraham. But there is no record of anything they said to one another on the journey—only that brief conversation in the garden, a little way from the hill of sacrifice: "My

21

Father, if it be possible, let this cup pass from me" (Matt 26:39). Apparently the answer Jesus received was the same one Abraham implies to Isaac: "The sacrifice must be carried out, my Son."

Like Isaac, Jesus carries the wood up the hill to the place of offering, until he is relieved of the burden by Simon of Cyrene. Like Isaac, Jesus is laid out upon the wood. And as the knife was raised over Isaac's breast, so the hammers are raised over the nails for Jesus.

But here our stories become very different. There is no rescue for Jesus—no last-minute voice from heaven to save him from the awful death—no substitutionary ram, no rescuing Elijah to take away the pain. The hammers descend, the nails pierce flesh, the cross is reared up against the sky. And Jesus cries out with the voice of a Son who has been abandoned by his Father: "My God, my God, why hast thou forsaken me?" (Matt 27:46). When the wife of Martin Luther complained about Gen 22, "Martin, I don't believe God would ask anyone to sacrifice his son," Luther replied, "But Katie, God did."

Given the love between father and son that shines through Gen 22 and just as surely through the passion story, we can only imagine what it cost God to hear his Son cry out to him. Someone once said, "If you wish to know how God Almighty feels . . . listen to the beating of your own heart, and then add to it infinity." Listen to the sounds of Abraham's sobs, as he raises the knife above Isaac. God stands off to the side of the cross, and hears his Son cry out to him. And God weeps, "O Jesus, my Son, my Son; O Jesus, my beloved Son!"

Just as the story of Isaac confronts us at first with a monstrous "Why?" so too the story of the crucifixion of our Lord raises the same troubling question. In our time, some have even said that the cross, with its blood and pain, was an unnecessary torture, perpetrated upon an innocent Son by a cruel and heartless Father.

The truth is, of course, that God had to send his beloved Son to share our blood- and pain-filled life. Indeed, God even had to send his Son to descend into our death, because that was the only way he could find all of us wandering children lost out here in the darkness. How far are we away from our Father's house, do you think? Three long days' journey, lost somewhere in our own private lands of Moriah? To save us, the Son of God had to come where we are, into our life of affliction and suffering, into our violent and death-dealing world. And only by sharing it and taking it upon himself could he triumph over it on Easter morn.

God really did mean that promise to Abraham. He truly meant to bring blessing on us all by means of the descendant of Abraham, Jesus Christ. Abraham's faith in the land of Moriah enabled God's long history of salvation to proceed, until God's promise of blessing and salvation was fulfilled in the death and resurrection of Jesus Christ.

❧ 4 ❦

"The LORD Is a Man of War"

EXODUS 15:1–21

Plumbing the Text

THIS PASSAGE RECORDS ISRAEL'S HYMNIC RESPONSE OF thanksgiving and praise to God's specific acts of salvation in Israel's history. It is a text for Easter Vigil in the three-year common lectionary. Most prominent in the passage is the celebration of God's acts in the exodus deliverance of Israel from Egypt, although God's later deeds of guiding the people through the wilderness (v. 13), of taking them across the Jordan (v. 16), and of leading them into the promised land to God's sanctuary (vv. 13, 17) are also celebrated.

The original song of praise, sung by Miriam the prophetess and sister of Aaron and by all the women (v. 21), probably formed the original response after the exodus deliverance. It is likely that this was later expanded into the text that we now have by the addition of the superscription to the song in v. 1. Some scholars have thought that the passage presupposes the existence of the temple, but that is not necessarily the case, and the entire song could be dated as early as the eleventh century B.C., while Miriam's song in v. 21 may be as early as the exodus event itself, which was in the thirteenth century B.C.

The events of the exodus, the wilderness wandering, and the conquest of the land form central articles of Israel's most ancient creeds (cf., e.g., Deut 26:5–9). Our passage's account of the exodus is fully consonant with the prose narrative of Exod 14. God is the sole actor in the exodus deliverance, and Israel has done nothing to deserve it (Exod 14:13–14). The water of the Sea of Reeds is driven back by the blast of God's breath, so that the people walk through the sea on dry land (15:8; 14:21). When God allows the waters to return to their accustomed flow, the pursuing Egyptian troops are drowned (14:27–28). Exodus 14:31 tells us that because of their deliverance, the people believed in the Lord, and this passage in Exod 15 forms, then, their responding song of faith. Strangely, there is no mention of Moses in the song. God is the sole rescuer, and it is his deeds that are celebrated, because finally it is his love for his people that has brought about their deliverance from bondage (cf. Deut 7:7–8; Exod 2:22–25).

In order to understand our passage fully, we must know more about how Israel understood the exodus from Egypt. First of all, the deliverance was seen by Israel as her *redemption*, that is, as the act whereby God bought her back out of slavery. Thus, vv. 13 and 16 state that God has "redeemed" Israel or "purchased" her. A redeemer in Israelite society was a relative who bought back one of his kin out of slavery (Lev 25:47–49). From the time of the exodus on, God was known as the Redeemer of Israel (e.g., Ps 35; Isa 63:16; Jer 50:34; cf. Deut 7:8; Mic 6:4, etc.), who had acknowledged the Israelites to be his family members. Indeed, the exodus is the central redemptive act by God in the Old Testament, paralleling our undeserved redemption from slavery to sin and death by the cross and resurrection of Christ in the New Testament (cf. Rom 5:8).

Second, it was this act of redemption that first made Israel a people. Exodus 12:38 tells us that Israel came out of Egypt a "mixed multitude" of various tribes and clans and backgrounds. It was not blood or soil or economics or any other human factor that bound them together. Rather, they became one people because they had all been redeemed together, just as that is the one tie that binds the church into a universal community, though it be made up of all sorts of races and genders and backgrounds. The unifying characteristic of the people of God is that they share a common redemption, and if they forget that redeeming act of God, they become "no people" (cf. Hos 1:9; 1 Pet 2:10).

Therefore, from the time of the exodus on, God was known as the Father of Israel (Deut 32:6; 1 Chron 29:10; Isa 63:16; 64:8; Jer 3:19; Mal 1:6; 2:10; Isa 45:9–11), and Israel was his adopted son (Exod 4:22–23; Jer 31:9, 20; Hos 11:1; cf. Deut 8:5; Isa 1:2). It is that theology to which Paul draws a parallel when he says in Gal 4:3–7 that those of us who have been redeemed by Christ are the adopted children of God, allowed to call God "Abba! Father!" and made heirs of the promises to the covenant people.

In celebrating the exodus redemption, as recorded in our passage, the Israelites were therefore praising God not only for their release from slavery but also because God had acknowledged them as his adopted children, become their Father, and made them and bound them together as a new people. They had the very founding events of their life to celebrate, just as Christians have all those same loving acts of God to celebrate.

Forming the Sermon

In v. 3 of our passage, the Lord who has done all of these saving deeds is called "a man of war," which could simply be read "warrior," as the NRSV has it. The Lord of the Bible is a warrior.

We do not like that title for God very well, because it does not fit our conceptions of God. Indeed, there is now a systematic effort in our churches to eliminate all militaristic language from the Bible and the church. We believe in peacemaking. Therefore, the hymn, "Onward Christian Soldiers" has been eliminated from our worship books, as have "The Battle Hymn of the Republic," which is based on the militaristic passage of Isa 63:1–6, and "March on, My Soul, with Might," which is a quote from Judg 5:21.

It cannot be denied that the Scriptures are full of battles and battle language. God is frequently described as the "LORD God of hosts," and "hosts" can refer to his heavenly armies or sometimes to the armies of Israel. The picture of the ideal Davidic messianic king includes his victory over all of his enemies because, as the Royal Psalm 144 states, God has trained the king's hands for war (v. 1; cf. Ps 18:34, 39, 48; 20:5–9; 21:8–13; 45:4–5; 89:22–23; 110:5–6; 132:18, all of which are Royal Psalms). Thus, the language of the Royal Psalm 110:1 is used of Christ in 1 Cor 15:25: "For he must reign until he has put all his enemies under his feet." The Lord Christ is engaged in a battle, and according to Matt 10:34 he has not come to bring peace but a sword.

The language of "The Holy War" also permeates the Scriptures. This concept refers to the fact that Israel's battles up until the time of David were fought according to fixed cultic rules. God was the principal contestant in the battle, fighting on behalf of his endangered people with supernatural means. He would bring panic over the enemy, turn their swords against one another, throw down great stones from heaven, bring darkness between the enemy and Israel, send thunder or earthquakes. Two of those means (the darkness, Exod 10:21–23, and the panic, Exod 14:24–25) are found in the story of the exodus. God is, indeed, a warrior in both Old Testament and New (cf. Rev), and, perhaps by ignoring that witness, we have refused to hear the full testimony of the gospel.

What is emphasized about God here in our passage in Exod 15? The answer is evident: his power. God is Israel's "strength" and can therefore be her salvation (v. 2). God's right hand is "glorious in power" (v. 6). He overthrows the adversaries and shatters the enemy (vv. 6–7), consuming them like stubble (v. 7). He is "majestic," doing glorious deeds and wonders (v. 11). Because of the greatness of his arm, the nations tremble and are still before him (vv. 14–16). God has been able to deliver his people from slavery, lead them through the wilderness, and bring them into the promised land because he has the power to do so.

27

Throughout the Scriptures, it is that power that distinguishes the Lord from all other gods (v. 11). Other gods are powerless; they cannot do anything. For example, the gods of Egypt were helpless to protect their people from the plagues sent by the Lord (Exod 12:12). Second Isaiah has a devastating portrayal of the gods of Babylonia who, because they themselves have to be carried about, cannot carry and save their people as the Lord has done (Isa 46).

Unlike other deities, the God of the Bible has all power over nature and history. He can roll back the waters of the Reed Sea or punish his disobedient people with drought. He can thwart the empires of Egypt and Assyria, or use Cyrus of Persia as his servant. He can call the universe into being and can kill or make alive. And because he can do these things, Israel confessed that he alone was God.

> Thus says the LORD, the King of Israel
>   and his Redeemer, the LORD of hosts:
> "I am the first and I am the last;
>   besides me there is no god." (Isa 44:6)

We should remember this when we are toying with the many deities worshiped in our time. Can they bring forth events in the natural world or in human history? Can they defeat death?

The God of the Bible is assuredly a God of love. But if he does not have the power to make his love effective in human life, then he and his purpose for the world are at the mercy of sinful human beings. What would have been the outcome, for example, if the Lord had not had power over the Pharaoh of Egypt in the time of the exodus? What would have been the fate of exiled Israel if the Babylonians alone had been in charge? Or most telling of all, in what could we put our faith if Herod's or Pilate's sentence of death for Jesus had been the final word? Everywhere throughout the Bible, God is a God of love who has the power to bring forth the results of his love. And this passage in Exod 15 celebrates the strength of that love manifested toward Israel.

That God is a God of power and love should be a comforting thought, for in our text we read the result of the

28

contest between God and empire, between the King of Israel and Pharaoh Rameses II of Egypt. That is what the whole exodus story is about—God the Ruler confronting human rule, just as thirteen centuries later in the salvation history Christ the King confronted the power of Rome (cf. John 18:33–19:22).

Those confrontations still take place in our time: God in Christ set against Mao Tse-tung and Adolph Hitler; the church set against persecution in Central America and China and Africa; indeed, every Christian in every place confronted by the overwhelming power of darkness and evil. As Ephesians says,

> . . . we are not contending against flesh and blood, but against the principalities, against the powers, against the world rulers of this present darkness, against the spiritual hosts of wickedness in the heavenly places. (Eph 6:12)

There is a vast monster of evil let loose in our world, and it takes many forms. As Martin Luther King Jr. wrote of our text, "Egypt symbolized evil in the form of humiliating oppression, ungodly exploitation, and crushing domination."[1] But evil can find its home in troubled hearts as well as in tyrannical nations. It can haunt the streets of our towns as well as the battlefields of the world. It can wreak death and the destruction of souls and misery beyond imagining, and you and I have only the power of the God in whom we trust to combat and put down that evil. "Take the whole armor of God," Ephesians continues, "that you may be able to withstand in the evil day, and having done all, to stand" (6:13).

Is it not comforting, then, to know that the Lord is mightier than any evil, that he cannot be defeated by any principality or power, that he could by his majestic strength deliver Israel from the clutches of Pharaoh as he delivered Jesus Christ from the grip of death?

The peaceful, benign gods of beauty and quiet that we imagine for ourselves in our day and age are quite powerless before the violence and wrong of our sin-pocked planet. But the Lord is not powerless. He is the warrior who can defeat every evil enemy and prevent anything in life or death from separating us from his love (Rom 8:39). "The LORD will reign for ever and ever," says our text (v. 18), and indeed, he has and does and always will.

Notes

1. *Strength to Love* (Philadelphia: Fortress, 1981), 73.

⚘ 5 ⚘

"Let Not God Speak to Us"

EXODUS 19:9–20; 20:18–21

*I*F WE STUDY THE THEOPHANIES OR APPEARANCES OF GOD in the Old Testament, it becomes impossible to trivialize or sentimentalize God's nature. For that reason, it is absolutely necessary that preachers present to their congregations the portrayal of God that we have here in Exod 19 and 20 and similar passages.

Plumbing the Text

The two texts we are examining bracket the account of the giving of the Ten Commandments in Exod 20:1–17, and thus they put those commandments in their proper hermeneutical context. Here we have the witness to the only time in the Old Testament when the whole people of God hears God speaking.

Israel is at Mt. Sinai after her merciful deliverance from slavery in Egypt and God's initial guidance of her across the wilderness. God has told Moses of his desire to enter into covenant with his people, in order that they may be his "kingdom of priests" and his "holy nation" (Exod 19:5–6). The Ten Commandments will form the content of that covenant, setting forth Israel's covenant obligations to this God who has redeemed her. But before the covenant is "cut" in Exod 24, these passages serve to validate the presence of God

with the people and the appointment of Moses as the mediator between God and the people.

God gives ample warning of his descent to Sinai. The
absolutely Holy One is going to come into the midst of
profane human beings, and so all normal activities of the
profane realm must cease, including marital relations (v. 15).
Clothes must be washed clean (v. 10), the people consecrated
or set apart (vv. 10, 14), and the mountain fenced off as God's
space, to be touched by no one (vv. 12–13). Holy power is
coming into the midst of the people, and they are warned that
it can kill them.

All religions have some sense of holy power, that is, of
the awesome and yet fascinating power that belongs to the
sacred realm and that is totally other than all profane and
human power. Therefore all religions have cults and rites
whereby the holy is prevented from mixing with and harming
the profane realm of life.

In the Old Testament, holy power is connected with the
ark of the covenant, the base of God's throne, and when
Uzzah touches the ark, he dies (2 Sam 6:6–7). The priestly
writers maintain that whoever touches the altar has holy
power transmitted to him (Exod 29:37), and Ezek 44:19 says
that whoever touches the holy garments of the priests becomes holy. Perhaps the clearest example for us, however, is
found in Mark's story of the woman who had a flow of blood
for twelve years (Mark 5:25–34) and who sought healing
from Jesus. "If I touch even his garments, I shall be made
well," she says. And when she touches and is healed, Mark
says, "And Jesus, perceiving that power had gone forth from
him, immediately turned . . . " Holy power is active, and it
can heal or kill or make alive. So the people must be pro-
tected at Sinai from the overwhelming holy power of God's
presence.

When God descends to the mountain his actual being is
not seen. Rather, simply the cosmic disturbances that accompany his presence are described, and that is always the way in
the Bible. Exodus 24:11 says that Moses, Aaron, Nadab,
Abihu, and seventy elders eat and drink with God on Sinai in

what could be described as the first Lord's Supper, and "they beheld God." But only his surroundings are described, as is true also in Isa 6:1–4. Only Moses, the special prophet of the Lord, beholds "the form of the LORD" (Num 12:8; but cf. Exod 33:20–23), while Ezekiel sees something like his appearance (Ezek 1:28). Human beings cannot see God and live (Exod 33:20).

God's person is hidden in cloud and fire, and his descent is accompanied by thunder and lightnings, earthquake and trumpet, all cosmic manifestations that are associated with God's presence on earth (cf. Ps 97:1–5; Isa 64:1–3; Ezek 1:4, 13; Hab 3:3–6, 9–11, et al.). The God who descends to Sinai can make the earth tremble and the mountains smoke (Ps 104:32; 144:5) or melt the earth over which he is Lord (Ps 46:6; Amos 9:5). He can cleave the ground with rivers (Hab 3:9) and control the chaotic deep (Ps 104:5–9; Heb 3:10). He can ride on the wings of the wind and make fire and flame his servants (Ps 104:4). The poets and prophets of the Old Testament simply strain at the bounds of language to depict the awesomeness of God. But it is that indescribable deity who wishes to enter into covenant with his people.

God speaks to Moses in thunder (cf. John 12:28–30; Ps 29:3–9), and when the terrified people hear it, they beg Moses to speak God's words to them instead, to become their mediator of the Word of God (Exod 20:10; Deut 5:22–27). Moses' ministry as the medium of God's word is validated (Exod 20:19). Thus, the commandments that he gives from God in the Decalogue are affirmed to be genuine words of the Lord.

Moses' reply to the people's terror is, "Do not fear," which is frequently the assurance that follows a divine approach. ("Fear not, for behold I bring you good tidings of great joy . . ." Luke 2:10 KJV; cf. Gen 15:1; 26:24; Exod 14:13; Matt 14:17, etc.) God has let the people hear him speak, Moses explains, in order that they may "fear" him, that is, obey him (v. 20) according to the commandments that God gives to the people through Moses.

Forming the Sermon

There is probably no better corrective for our worship of
God than these passages in Exod 19 and 20. We are very casual
in our worship services these days. The preacher says "Good
morning" in a very folksy fashion. Often in contemporary
services, guitar music and modern popular religious songs
constitute the praise; and the attitude and dress of the
congregation are casual and everyday. In traditional services,
a lack of earnestness can exist; the prayers are recited rou-
tinely, half of the congregation does not sing, and a few
elderly nod off for a morning nap.

Consequently we do not like this passage in Exod 19
very well. First of all, we do not like its emphasis on a
mediator. A woman friend said to me one time, "There is
something wrong if I can't approach God and speak to him
directly without a mediator." I did not argue with her at the
time, but the whole point is that there *is* something wrong!
We are sinners, blotched and blemished with the wrong and
evil of a profane and sinful world, and like Israel, if we
approach the holy God in our sin, we will be destroyed. Israel
knew that, and so she begged Moses to be her spokesman
before God and to mediate the words of God to her. And we
now pray every prayer in the name of and for the sake of Jesus
Christ, who is our mediator of the Word of God and our
justification. Apart from Christ's mediation, we literally do
not have a prayer.

Beyond that, however, we do not like the picture of an
awesome God that is revealed to us in Exod 19 and 20, with
all of its fire and smoke, its thunder and the mountain quaking. We much prefer what we consider to be the correction of
that picture in Heb 12:18–24.

> For you have not come to what may be touched, a blazing fire,
> and darkness, and gloom, and a tempest, and the sound of a
> trumpet, and a voice whose words made the hearers entreat
> that no further messages be spoken to them. For they could
> not endure the order that was given, "If even a beast touches
> the mountain, it shall be stoned." Indeed, so terrifying was the

sight that Moses said, "I tremble with fear." But you have come to . . . Jesus, the mediator of a new covenant . . .

Our conception of coming to Jesus is of a meeting of gentleness and peacefulness, forgiveness and love, and not blazing fire and thunder and trembling. "Amazing grace, how sweet the sound." We believe that our Lord is in our midst when we worship and that we have absolutely nothing to fear from his presence. We can welcome him as a friend, a lover, a tender shepherd of his sheep, and we can bask in the sweetness of a "closer walk" with him.

The result of having such a one-sided conception of the divine presence is that we then do not take God's commandments very seriously. Our Lord reaffirms the Ten Commandments as instruction for the Christian life (Mark 10:17–20) and then gives us multiple teachings about living a life of righteousness in him (cf. Matt 5–7). But our kindly, friendly God, so many think, is really not very serious. Commandments can be broken at will, and God will forgive. He is a gentle God, a forgiving God who understands our difficulties.

The truth is that the same formidable God who descended to Sinai in smoke and fire is also the God and Father of our Lord Jesus Christ. When God descended to the Israelites at Sinai, he brought with him that covenant demand. "You shall have no other gods besides me." And Jesus, who is present in our worship of him, lays upon us that same undivided loyalty. "Take up your cross and follow me"; "I am the way, and the truth, and the life." "Not everyone who says to me, 'Lord, Lord,' shall enter the kingdom of heaven, but he who does the will of my Father who is in heaven."

In similar fashion, the awe-inspiring mystery that surrounded the Lord when he descended to the mount still surrounds our knowledge of God in Jesus Christ. That he should love the likes of you and me, that he should guard our every moment, that he should number the hairs on our heads and listen to our mumbled and selfish prayers—that is surely beyond comprehension. More than that, it is difficult to comprehend that such a God should give up his only begotten Son and have him nailed to a tree just because he wants all people to have forgiveness and life forever. Can you or I encompass in thought the depth of such love? Can we peer to the heart of God and understand his compassion?

> See, from his head, his hands, his feet,
> Sorrow and love flow mingled down!
> Did e'er such love and sorrow meet?
> Or thorns compose so rich a crown?[1]

That for us is still the central and most important mystery in our universe. And at the foot of the cross we can only stand in reverent awe, or approach Christ's supper in wonder, hearing that beyond all reason and imagination, the life of Christ is poured out to us by the Spirit in the symbols of bread and wine.

As for the power that caused Mt. Sinai to quake and that can still shake our world, surely that power was manifested in Jesus Christ our Lord. The blind received their sight, the lame walked, lepers were cleansed, the deaf were given hearing, and the dead were raised. But more than that, Christ wrestled with the forces of chaos and death and hell itself and now stands in our midst—alive! And his power can still transform human beings and make of them totally new creatures. The God of power who descended to Sinai is incarnate in Jesus Christ.

The result is that we read at the end of the New Testament passage in Hebrews of Christ's final victory.

> You have come to Mount Zion and to the city of the living God, the heavenly Jerusalem, and to innumerable angels in festal gathering, and to the assembly of the first-born who are enrolled in heaven, and to a judge who is God of all, and to the spirits of just men made perfect, and to Jesus . . ." (Heb 12:22–24)

That is the picture of the Kingdom of God, the heavenly Zion and Jerusalem, that will also be established on earth, in which the final victory will be won by Christ and God will be all in all. The God of Sinai, the God of power, of blazing fire and smoke and earthquake, is finally the God who has the might to establish the Kingdom of Heaven on earth.

Such is the God whom we enter to worship when we walk into our sanctuaries—the God of Sinai incarnated in our Lord Jesus Christ. Therefore, as Hebrews tells us, "Let us offer to God acceptable worship, with reverence and awe; for our God is a consuming fire" (Heb 12:28–29).

Notes

1. Third stanza of "When I Survey the Wondrous Cross." Isaac Watts, 1707.

❧ 6 ❧

"The Skin of Moses' Face Shone"

EXODUS 34:29–35

THIS IS THE STATED OLD TESTAMENT LESSON FOR TRANS-
figuration Sunday in Cycle C of the three-year common
lectionary, and it has a direct connection with both 2 Cor
3:7–18 and 4:6. It is paired with the account of the Transfiguration in Luke 9 and can be linked with v. 29 of that gospel
text. However, Matt 17:2 furnishes a more exact connection.

Plumbing the Text

The story tells of Moses' descent from talking with God
on Mt. Sinai. Israel's worship of the golden calf has caused a
deep rupture between God and his covenant people (Exod
32, 33). Nevertheless, God graciously enters into covenant
with Israel once again and gives Moses the covenant commands that the people are to follow (Exod 34:10–28). These
include not only the Ten Commandments (34:28) but also
the Ritual Decalogue concerning the people's worship that is
found in Exod 34:10–26. Moses descends the holy mountain
in order to deliver God's renewed covenant commands to his
people.

The emphasis of our particular text is not on the
commandments, however, but on the fact that Moses' face

shines from talking with God. When the people see this phenomenon, they are filled with fear (v. 30). Moses nevertheless draws them to himself and delivers the words of God (vv. 31, 32).

The text makes it clear that this is a continuing event, not limited to this one time. Whenever Moses talks with God (apparently not on the mountain but in the tent of meeting described in 33:7–11; cf. 34:34), Moses' face afterward shines, so that he must put a veil over his countenance in between revelations. When he delivers the words of God to the people, he removes the veil, signifying the fact that he is in truth the Lord's messenger. But after he has delivered the word, the veil is donned once again.

'Forming the Sermon

Perhaps many of you have seen Michelangelo's statue of Moses or at least a miniature copy of it. In the statue, Moses is holding the tablets of the law, but on his head, Moses also has two small horns. That comes from the fact that the verb for "to shine" *(qeran)* in the Hebrew text of Exodus could also be translated "horn" *(qeren),* and that latter was the reading from the Vulgate that Michelangelo followed. But no, the text is clear. "The skin of Moses' face shone" (34:35).

What a strange phenomenon! To understand it, we must talk about the nature of God. We have often heard the phrase, "the glory of God," and we have a vague notion that it is somehow connected with light. We all know the Christmas story where "The glory of the Lord shone round about them, and they were sore afraid" (Luke 2:9 KJV). But what exactly is the glory of the Lord?

In the Scriptures, God's glory has one of two meanings. The basic meaning of the verb *kabed,* to have glory, is "to be heavy." And in that usage, God's glory is his "weight" in the community or world, the esteem and honor in which he is held. Thus when the Psalmist asks us to "ascribe to the LORD the glory due his name" (Ps 96:8), he is calling us to give honor and esteem to God for all of his wonderful deeds.

The other meaning of the glory of God is much different,
however, and it is this meaning with which we are concerned
in our text. God's glory in this second meaning has to do with
his Person, and it signifies the visible form in which God
reveals himself on earth.

Sometimes such form takes on the appearance of a
storm, or at least is accompanied by elements that we would
attribute to a thunderstorm. In Ps 97, for example, it is said
that "clouds and thick darkness are round him" (v. 2), "fire
goes before him, and burns up his adversaries round about"
(v. 3), "his lightnings lighten the world" (v. 4), and "the
mountains melt like wax" before him (v. 5). In Ezek 1 there
are a storm, clouds, fire, lightning, and a deafening noise
like a cloudburst. All are expressions of the overwhelming
manifestation of God's presence on earth. (Cf. the account
of God's descent to the top of Mt. Sinai in Exod 19:16–19.)
For this reason, some have mistakenly believed that God
was first known as a storm God, connected with the holy
mountain, Horeb or Sinai. But many of the texts having to
do with the glory of the Lord have nothing to do with
meteorology.

In our text, which comes from the Priestly Writers, the
glory of the Lord is a fiery light phenomenon, the glow of
which is then reflected on Moses' skin because Moses is
privileged to speak to God "face to face" (cf. Exod 33:11;
Deut 34:10). It is this fiery light that fills the tabernacle on
Mt. Sinai, signifying the Lord's constant presence in the
midst of his people (Exod 40:34–38). However, the fiery light
is surrounded by a cloud because no ordinary human being,
except Moses, can bear to look at God's fiery glory. No one
can see God and live (Exod 33:20). Indeed, in the wonderful
story of Exod 33:20–23 even Moses cannot see God's face: he
is allowed only to glimpse God's back. The two traditions,
Exod 33:11 from the Priestly Writers and Exod 33:20 from the
Yahwist Writer, are somewhat contradictory, but in both, human inability to see God is emphasized: Moses must veil his
face from his fellow Israelites because they cannot bear to see
even the reflection of God's glory.

40

In the vision of the prophet Ezekiel, the fiery glory takes on something like the appearance of a human form (see the exposition on Ezek 1:26–28), and the prophet is so overwhelmed by the vision that he falls prostrate and then sits in stunned silence for seven days (Ezek 3:15). Anyone who sees God's glory is overwhelmed and made fearful by it, like the shepherds in Luke's Christmas story who "were sore afraid" (Luke 2:9 KJV).

Further, it is said in Ezekiel that God in his glory dwells in the Holy of Holies in the temple, but because of Israel's sin against him, his glory departs from the temple (Ezek 10:4; 11;23) and will not return until there is a new temple in the eschatological time (Ezek 43:1–5).

The skin of Moses' face shines with the reflected light of the fiery glory of the Lord. The story emphasizes Moses' authority to deliver God's commandments to the people. Moses has received the commandments directly from God himself, and he faithfully passes on the words of God to the people over whom God has given him charge. He fulfills the prophetic function, and he could very well use the prophetic phrase, "Thus says the LORD." The Mosaic commandments are to be taken with utter seriousness, because they come from the Lord of heaven and earth.

The Apostle Paul, however, uses this passage from Exod 34 differently in 2 Cor 3:7–18. He knows after his conversion that the law has only a fading splendor, because fulfillment of the law cannot bring salvation. Once the law had a splendor about it. It was intended to bring life, but it brought only death instead (2 Cor 3:6), because in fulfilling the law, human beings were relying on their own works rather than on God. Therefore Paul maintains that Moses veiled his face in order that the Israelites would not see its splendor fading (2 Cor 3:13).

Further, Paul writes that not only Moses' face was veiled. The minds of the Israelites were veiled too when they heard the law, and the minds of Paul's fellow Jews are still veiled when they read the Old Testament, because they did not accept Christ and they do not find Christ in the Old Testament.

41

Only "in Christ," only through faith in him and participation in him is the veil removed and the law heard correctly (2 Cor 3:14–16). Then the law is understood in the Spirit, and then the Spirit gives freedom (2 Cor 3:17). It is in the face of Christ that we find the true glory of God (2 Cor 4:6), and it is in the Spirit of Christ that the commandments of God lead to freedom and life.

We Christians know that Christ is the fulfillment of the law, fulfilling all righteousness (cf. Matt 3:15), and rendering to God that perfect obedience and trust that we always have been unable to give to God by our own will and work. By faith in Christ Jesus, we are freed from the works of the law and given "the glorious liberty of the children of God" (Rom 8:21). We no longer have to work diligently in order to win our own acceptance and salvation in the eyes of God, making sure that we fulfill every little jot and tittle of righteousness, and worrying that we somewhere might have fallen short. We are freed from such anxiety and vain striving, because we have been counted good in the eyes of God through his gracious gift of his Son.

And yet, Christ lays commandments upon us just as Moses did upon the Israelites. In fact, Jesus repeats some of the commandments that Moses gave and makes them incumbent upon us. For example, the Ten Commandments are still to guide our Christian lives (cf. Mark 10:17–21), and love of God and neighbor from Deut 6:5 and Lev 19:18—both laws from Moses—are still in Jesus' words made the principle demands of God upon us (Mark 12:28–31). What then? Are we delivered from obedience to the law or not?

Some persons in our time have so misinterpreted the Scriptures that they have maintained that the Christian has no command to follow from Jesus or anyone else. And the results have been the chaos and evil that we find in our society and that we read about in the morning headlines.

The New Testament is clear. God expects from us obedience to the commands of his Son. But that obedience is to be given, not in order to win our salvation and eternal life from God, but because Christ has already won that eternal

42

salvation for us by his death and resurrection. Indeed, if it were not for the Spirit of Christ working in us, we would not be able to be trusting and obedient. But Christ's Spirit gives us the power. Christ working in us enables us to be faithful and to do the good.

Christ's commandments, then, are God's gracious guides about how to live and walk in this new life that Christ has made possible for us. God does not leave us to stumble around in the dark, wondering what we are to do in our Christian lives, and making up the rules as we go along. No, God gives us guidance through the commands of the New Testament. He says to us, "This is the way. Walk in it. This is the way you can have abundant life." And out of gratitude and thanksgiving for that marvelous gift, we rely on Christ's Spirit, and we obey.

We have seen "the light of the knowledge of God in the face of Jesus Christ" (2 Cor 4:6). God in his untouchable glory has stooped to our condition and walked among us in Jesus Christ. And by his Spirit working in us, says Paul, we can be changed into his likeness "from one degree of glory to another" (2 Cor 3:18). Christ's Spirit can make us good, as he was wholly good. And in that Spirit there is life and freedom and eternal life in the company of the Father.

❦ 7 ❧

The Bronze Serpent

NUMBERS 21:4–9

*I*N PREPARATION FOR WRITING THIS BOOK, I ASKED CLERGY
and lay acquaintances what passages in the Old Testament
bothered them. One lay women, who was thoroughly ac-
quainted with the Scripture, replied, "the bronze serpent."

This is a rather brief text in Numbers, but reference to
it prevails even into the time of King Hezekiah's reform
(727–698 B.C.), according to 2 Kgs 18:4, and it takes on
christological importance because Jesus compares his eleva-
tion on the cross to Moses' lifting up the serpent in the
wilderness (John 3:14–15). Thus, it may be a passage on
which we wish to preach (especially since it is the stated Old
Testament lesson for the fourth Sunday in Lent in Cycle B).

Plumbing the Text

The story in the text is straightforward, embodying the
pattern of Israel's murmuring and rebellion in the wilderness
that is so frequent throughout the wilderness material (cf.
Exod 16:1–3; Num 11:1–3, 4–6; 14:1–3). The people com-
plain to both Moses and God that they have no food or water
and that they loathe the manna with which God is feeding
them daily (cf. Num 11:6). Because of their lack of faith and
gratitude, God sends fiery serpents that bite and kill some of
the people. The people repent, Moses intercedes for them

before the Lord, and God provides the means whereby they may be cured. Moses erects a bronze serpent on a pole, and anyone who is bitten and looks at it lives. This pattern of complaint, judgment, repentance, intercession, and succor is frequent in the wilderness traditions.

The text reflects many ancient traditions. For instance, many cultures have understood the serpent to be a symbol of healing. The Greek healing god, Asklepios, is said to have appeared in the form of a serpent, and still today our medical symbol includes a serpent. Further, there is even in the Old Testament the hint of the ancient belief that one could annul the power of a dangerous creature by making an image of it and rendering some kind of worship to it (1 Sam 5–6). We might conclude, therefore, that this text embodies ancient magical and superstitious beliefs and has very little to do with normative biblical faith. Such is not the case, as will be shown below.

A few things about these serpents should be noted. God sends "fiery serpents" among the people, but it is a "bronze serpent" that Moses puts up on a pole. Perhaps the two are identified because of the similarity between the color of bronze and that of fire. "Fiery serpents and scorpions" are said to inhabit the wilderness in Deut 8:15. There is also reference to "flying serpents" in Isa 14:29, which are worse than ordinary serpents. The flying seraphim that Isaiah sees in his vision in Isa 6:2 have long been said to be serpentine in form. It may be, therefore, that the "fiery serpents" of our text are to be understood as somewhat supernatural creatures sent by God to punish the people, although that is speculation.

Forming the Sermon

Any congregation is likely, upon hearing this text, to dismiss it as a piece of ancient superstition. Whoever heard of being magically cured by looking at a bronze sculpture on a pole?

We are not too far from such superstition in our day, however: "knock on wood," "never walk under a ladder," and "don't let a black cat cross your path." There are many who think that if they wear a copper bracelet they will be cured of cancer. There are a lot of people who believe that a pyramid form carries with it a special power to make them whole. We have lucky objects of all kinds, don't we—rabbits' feet, horseshoes, heaven knows what all? And I have even encountered people on airplane flights who think that if a clergy person is on the plane, it cannot possibly crash. We are not very far from the ancient superstition that we think is found in this text.

The truth is, however, that this text does not represent some ancient magical superstition, for it does not say that the bronze serpent by itself has the power to heal the Israelites. It is not the presence of the bronze figure that leads to the healing of the people.

Indeed, during the later eighth-century religious reform of King Hezekiah of Judah, he destroys the bronze serpent that has been kept in the temple for centuries, because the people have turned the figure into an idol and are burning incense to it. They think the serpent has divine power in itself to help them, just as people in our day think some pyramid has divine power, or some copper bracelet can cure them. The thing itself has been turned into an idol.

There are persons in our time who make an idol out of the Bible or a church sanctuary or a bronze cross—out of anything that seems to them to be holy. So the Bible, for example, is turned into a magical charm that the bride carries down the aisle on her wedding day. It protects her, even if she never reads it.

All of that is far from what our text says. Why are the people healed in this story from the book of Numbers? They are healed, first of all, because God provides them a way to be healed. And then second, their cure comes because they obey the Word of God and do what he tells them to do. In short, their cure comes from their faith in God and from their faithful obedience to his instructions.

That is why our Lord Jesus can then use this text as a foreshadowing of his crucifixion. As Moses lifted up the serpent in the wilderness, so Jesus will be lifted up on the cross, to draw all people to himself. But the benefit of the cross—its power to forgive our sins and to give us eternal life—then can be had by us only as we come to Christ in trust and obedience. The sacrifice is made for us and for all people; the cross is there; the deed has been done; God has given his only Son. But now we must respond to that gift. We must appropriate it in faith and obedience. We must make its benefits our own, by the commitment of our hearts and lives to Jesus Christ our Savior. As Moses lifted up the serpent in the wilderness, our Lord is lifted up on his cross, and whoever believes in Jesus may have forgiveness and eternal life.

❧ 8 ❧

Excursus: The Ban

DEUTERONOMY 20:10–18 AND CONQUEST TEXTS

*I*T IS DOUBTFUL THAT ANY PREACHER WILL WANT TO PREACH a sermon on the texts that deal with the ancient ritual of the ban, or *herem* in the Hebrew. Nevertheless, when I ask persons what Old Testament texts disturb them, those having to do with the ban are frequently mentioned. Therefore in a book having to do with difficult passages, it seems wise to deal with the subject.

Examining the Texts

The ban was a part of what scholars have named Israel's "Holy War." During the period of the conquest, of the Judges, and up through the time of Saul's reign, Israel's wars were conducted according to strict cultic requirements. For that reason, scholars have termed them "holy" or "sacral" wars.

In the rituals of such wars, Israel's citizen troops and weapons were consecrated to the Lord and the camp was kept ritually pure. Before the troops went into battle, a sacrifice was offered to God, who was considered to be the Divine Warrior, fighting on behalf of Israel with his heavenly hosts and defeating the enemy by supernatural means. The Lord would send lightning, storm (Judg 5:20–22), and earthquake (Josh 6:20?), and cause panic to fall upon the enemy (Deut 2:25; Judg 7:22). Thus, the decisive factor was not the size of Israel's army (cf.

Judg 7) but faith in the power of the Lord who had delivered the people out of bondage in Egypt (Deut 20:1–4). When God won the battle, then all war booty and conquered peoples were the property of the Lord, who was the true Victor. The ban or *herem* is based on God's complete possession of the enemy with his goods. The destruction of these things is a sacrifice to the Lord. Sometimes a city was allowed to surrender peacefully (Deut 20:10) or the ban stipulated only the destruction of enemy warriors (Deut 20:13–15) but more often total annihilation was required (Deut 20:16).

The Book of Joshua records that Joshua's troops exercised the ban toward the cities of Jericho (Josh 6:21), Makkeda, Libnah, Lachish, Eglon, Hebron, and Debir, in the southern part of the conquest of Canaan (Josh 10:22–40), although Josh 11:13 adds some other evidence. Numbers 21:13 adds Hormah to the list (cf. Judg 1:17), and Jabesh-Gilead is named in Judg 21:11. The story of Achan in Josh 7 adds the defeat of Ai, while Deut 20:10–15 states that the Canaanite cities and populations that were utterly destroyed were those that would not make peace with the invading Israelites.

There is, however, a good deal of evidence to question whether the ban was ever carried out to the extent given in the records of the conquest and of Judges. As Walter Rast has stated, "whatever we may have in the way of historical memory in the book of Joshua, it has often been put through the sieve of later interpretation."[1]

For example, there is no archaeological evidence that the village of Ai suffered destruction during the period of Israel's entrance into the land. The hand of the exilic Deuteronomic Editors is evident throughout the Book of Joshua, and the repeated statement that Joshua "utterly destroyed everything that breathed" (Josh 10:40; 11:14; Deut 20:16) has been widely recognized as the Deuteronomic Editors' judgment. Similarly, the account of the ban in Judges occurs only in the Deuteronomic Editors' framework of the book (Judg 1:17; 21:11), and Deut 20:10–20 is the Deuteronomic Editors' reading back into Israel's history from the time of the Babylonian exile.

The Deuteronomic Editors had several purposes in mind. First, because they always viewed Israel's life as a whole, they gave the impression that the conquest of the promised land was swift and complete, and that the Canaanite population was eliminated (Josh 11:20–23), whereas Judg 1, an older independent account of the conquest, points out that such was not the case.

Second, the Deuteronomic Editors' were giving a theological account of why Israel was sent into exile. God had fought for Israel and given her the promised land through his mighty deeds of war. But Israel forgot God's saving acts on her behalf and went after other gods. Therefore, she deserved the punishment of the exile.

Third, to avoid future punishment in her return from exile, the Deuteronomic Editors were emphasizing to Israel the absolute necessity of strict loyalty to the Lord alone. All Canaanite influences, gods, and worshipers were to be totally eschewed by Israel in order that she not be drawn away from her total loyalty to the one God, Yahweh. Israel was not to have any other god besides him (Deut 5:7), whom she was to love with all her heart and soul and might (Deut 6:4–5). To remove the temptation to go after the other gods of the Canaanites, early Israel therefore was said to have exterminated Canaanite cities and their inhabitants.

As Walter Rast has further pointed out, however,[2] had such been the actual case, Israel never would have been drawn into the idolatry that both Deuteronomy and the prophets continually condemn, and the Assyrian and Babylonian exiles never would have been necessary. It was not because the population of Canaan was eliminated by the ban that Israel fell into idolatry. Rather, it was precisely because Israel lived in and among the Canaanite population after her entrance into the land. The fertility gods and goddesses of Canaan tempted Israel to seek the sources of her life in them rather than in the one God, Yahweh. We can therefore question whether the distasteful practice of the ban ever actually took place.

Having said that, we must nevertheless reckon with some historical exercise of the ban, because it lies behind the story of Achan in Judg 7, and the defiance of its ritual furnishes the background of both accounts of the rejection of Saul as Israel's king in 1 Sam 13 and 15. Indeed, Jesus quotes the words of Samuel to Saul, found in 1 Sam 15:22 (Matt 9:13; 12:7), "To obey is better than sacrifice," and that thought finds an echo in multiple passages of the Old Testament (cf. Ps 40:6–8; 51:16–17; Isa 1:11–15, and especially Hos 6:6). Obedience to God, no matter how onerous, is preferred to all other sacrifice. In the words of Hos 6:6, God demands "steadfast love," that is, covenant faithfulness to his commands.

A Possible Sermon

Our Lord, however, changes the wording of the command. Jesus says, "I desire mercy *(eleos)* and not sacrifice"— mercy even toward one's enemies. And true faith, therefore, becomes a matter not of eliminating one's enemies with all their foreign deities and worship practices, but of living in their idolatrous midst and yet holding fast in faith to the one God who is Lord of all.

Perhaps that is the sermon that needs to be preached from these texts, for certainly in our time we live in the midst of idolatrous populations. The test of our trust in the Lord, therefore, is whether we can hold fast to his will and Person in the face of all the temptations to find the source and sustenance of our life from other false deities that seek our loyalty, whether they be man-made, natural, or supernatural.

Notes

1. Walter E. Rast, "Joshua," in *Harper's Bible Commentary* (ed. James L. Mays; San Francisco: Harper & Row, 1988), 236a.
2. Ibid., 239a.

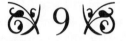

9

Moses Forbidden to Enter the Land

DEUTERONOMY 34:1–12

*T*HIS IS THE STATED TEXT FOR THE THIRTIETH SUNDAY in Pentecost or Ordinary Time of Cycle A. It records Moses' death and brings to a close the Book of Deuteronomy.

Plumbing the Text

Moses is not allowed to enter Canaan, that land that the Lord promised to his forebears some five centuries earlier (Gen 12:7; 15:18–21; 17:8, etc.). Instead, Moses is allowed only to view the land from Moab, on the eastern side of the Jordan.

Moses climbs to the top of Mt. Nebo, which is a promontory in the Abarim range opposite Jericho. At that point he is 2,740 feet above sea level and 4,030 feet above the Dead Sea, whose northern tip lies far below him. At that point, he then crosses over a saddle to the top of Pisgah. Even as a very old man he has retained his physical vigor, as v. 7 of our text states.

When Moses has reached that high vantage point, the Lord shows him all of the promised land, which is laid out before his eyes: from the territory in the north where Dan will reside; southward through the future regions of Naphtali, Manasseh, and Ephraim; and then the southern regions where

Judah will settle; and farther south still, the desert of the Negeb and the place of Zoar beyond the southern end of the Dead Sea.[1] At the same time, the Lord tells Moses once again that he must not cross over the Jordan into the land with his fellow Israelites (cf. Deut 32:50).

Having seen the land toward which he has led his people for so many years, Moses dies and is buried in an unmarked grave (v. 6). His death is properly mourned for thirty days and the leadership of Israel passes to Joshua (v. 9; cf. Josh 1:1–9). In the closing words of the text, Moses is celebrated as the greatest of all the prophets (vv. 10–12).

Forming the Sermon

I suppose we rarely think of Moses as a prophet, but the Old Testament knows that he was not only a prophet; he was the greatest among all of the spokesmen and -women of God that lived in ancient Israel. According to Deut 18:15, Moses therefore became the model of all true prophets, and every prophet who came after him, especially Jeremiah, probably saw themselves in Moses' image.

Certainly Moses fulfilled all of the prophetic functions. He became the mediator of the Word of God to the Israelites when they were unable to stand before God's glory because of their sin (Deut 5:22–27). And like so many of the prophets who followed him, Moses constantly interceded for his people before God (cf. Jer 7:16; 11:14; 15:1; Amos 7:1–6). When the Israelites worshiped the golden calf at Mt. Sinai, it was Moses' intercessory prayer and ascetic pleading that turned aside God's wrath (Deut 9:13–21), just as it was the same strenuous intercession that constantly begged God's forgiveness in the days that followed (Deut 9:22–29; 10:10).

Similarly, like the other prophets who followed him, Moses was a suffering mediator for his people and took the people's sins upon himself. That was the reason why Moses was not allowed to enter the promised land. Israel had not trusted the Lord's promise to give them the land, and so taking their sin upon himself, Moses died outside of the land

53

in order that Israel might enter into it (Deut 1:37; 3:26; 4:21).[2] In Deut 3:23–28, Moses begs the Lord to allow him to cross the Jordan into Canaan, but the Lord says no, and Moses is given the task of suffering for the sake of his sinful people.

Throughout the Old Testament story, Moses is a towering figure, and as our text states in v. 10, there was not another prophet like him. Unlike any other prophet, Numbers tells us that Moses was allowed to behold the form of the Lord and to speak with him "mouth to mouth" (Num 12:6–8).

Moses was not divine, however, and so Deuteronomy makes a point of saying that no one knew where he was buried, because it did not want worship of the dead or pilgrimages to Moses' grave site. Israel was to worship one God and him alone.

By New Testament times there did arise in Israel the expectation that God would fulfill his promise in Deut 18:15 and raise up a prophet like Moses, whose coming would mark the inauguration of the new age of God. We read of that expectation repeatedly in the Gospel according to John (1:21, 25; 6:14; 7:40).

Peter, according to the Acts of the Apostles, knew and proclaimed that the new age had arrived (Acts 3:22–26; 7:37, 52). Peter preached that the prophet like Moses was Jesus Christ, who mediated the Word of God to the people, who interceded for them in prayer (cf. Luke 23:24, "Father, forgive them for they know not what they do," and Rom 8:34), and who took all of their sins upon himself that God might forgive and grant life eternal. Our Lord is much more than a prophet like Moses. In Jesus' face the glory of God himself has shone upon us, and he himself is the Word of God incarnate. But the prophet he also surely is, fulfilling the mediating, interceding, and suffering functions of those men and women of God who looked toward his coming.

When our Lord came, he began the new age of the Kingdom of God (cf. Mark 1:15; Luke 11:20). In his person, sin and death were defeated and the rule of God over all the earth was begun. But that kingdom has not yet come in its fullness. We still see in a mirror darkly and not face to face (1 Cor 13:12). There are still "wars and rumors of war" and "the end is not yet" (Mark 13:7). Nevertheless, we have a guarantee of that coming kingdom and of its salvation for us, writes Paul. The gift of the Spirit in our hearts is that guarantee (2 Cor 1:22), and because we have been given the free gift of the Spirit of Christ, we know that we shall inherit eternal life (2 Cor 5:5).

We are like Moses in our text, you see. We are on the way to the promised land of the kingdom. Our deliverance out of slavery, like Israel's redemption from Egypt, lies behind us. It was won by Christ's victory over sin and death at Calvary and on Easter morn. But right now, like Moses, we are allowed only to view the fulfillment of the promise out there ahead of us. We are still on our Nebos and Pisgahs. The kingdom has only been shown to us—shown in the glory of Jesus Christ. And we still journey toward the time when every knee has bowed and every tongue confessed that Christ is Lord of all, to the glory of God the Father.

But our salvation comes, good Christians, our salvation comes. Indeed, we are taught that we have a foretaste of it when we sit at the Lord's Supper. At that meal we participate in the body and blood of Christ (1 Cor 10:16), who is now risen to the right hand of the Father. And so we have a little foretaste of the coming resurrection and of that final messianic banquet, when the Kingdom of God has come on earth even as it is in heaven, and all the faithful are gathered together from north and south, east and west, to sit at table in the household of God and to enjoy him forever (cf. Matt 8:11).

Notes

1. The fact that later tribal boundaries are mentioned shows that this chapter was written later than the time of Moses, as does also the account of Moses' death. Scholars now know that the initial Book of Deuteronomy was the product of the seventh century B.C., while this chapter was added, probably about 550 B.C.

2. A separate tradition in Num 20:10–13 states that it was Moses' own sin that prevented him from entering the land, but the nature of that failing is obscure.

❧ 10 ❧

In the Days of the Judges

JUDGES 4:1–7

*T*HIS IS THE STATED OLD TESTAMENT TEXT FOR THE thirty-third Sunday in Pentecost or Ordinary Time in cycle A of the three-year lectionary. Coming as it does almost at the end of the church year, and representing the lectionary's sole reading from the Book of Judges, it is doubtful that the passage is used as the basis of a sermon very often. The time of the Judges is an important one in Israel's history, however, and the theology of the Book of Judges helps fill out the understanding of God that comes to us through the Old Testament. Preachers could therefore profitably employ this text.

Plumbing the Text

The time of the Judges falls in Israel's history between Israel's entrance into the promised land, about 1220 B.C., and the anointing of Saul as their first king, in 1020 B.C. It is the time when the tribes of Israel were united together only in a very loose federation. They came together only once every year (or perhaps every seven years) at a central shrine to renew their sole loyalty to the Lord in a covenant-renewal ceremony. The ark of the covenant, which was considered to be the base of God's throne, with God enthroned invisibly above it, was the central cult object at the shrine. And the tribes took turns furnishing a priest to minister at the shrine. Otherwise, however, they largely went their own separate ways. There was no permanence in leadership. As Judges states: "In those days there was no king in Israel; every man did what was right in his own eyes" (17:5; 21:25).

Theologically, the Book of Judges considers Israel's entrance into the promised land of Canaan to be a time of testing (Judg 3:1–4). God fulfilled his promises to his people to give them many descendants, to enter into covenant with them, and to give them a land to call their own (Gen 12:1–3, 7; 15:5; 17:7–8; Josh 23:14). But God also promised their forebear Abraham that through Abraham's descendants, God would bring blessing on all the families of the earth (Gen 12:3). Israel was chosen as the instrument through whom God could reverse the consequences of humanity's sin and turn sin's curse into blessing. Israel could be the medium of such blessing, however, only if she remained faithful to her God. Her entrance into the land and the realm of the Canaanite gods now was seen as the time of the testing of that faithfulness. Would Israel remain loyal to the Lord alone, or would she go after the fertility gods and goddesses of the Canaanites?

Certainly Israel faced new and hitherto unknown conditions when she settled into Canaan. Previously she had been a desert, wandering people, and her God had been known to her in the desert. But now Israel had to adapt to farming, and her question was, Did the Lord control the rain and the dew (cf. the story of Gideon's fleece, Judg 6:36–40), and could he give fertility to the crops, or were those to be sought only from the gods and goddesses of fertility that the Canaanites worshiped?

Further, in at least a partial sense, Israel now had emerged into the world of nations as a state among states. How therefore was she to govern her life, and who would defend her against the enemies that surrounded her? God had been her King and Protector in Egypt and through forty years of wandering in the wilderness. Could God give her the same security in the political turmoils of the region, or did she finally have to have a king who would unite her disparate tribes and go out before her in battle (cf. 1 Sam 8)? The stories of the Judges are concerned with both of these issues.

There is a recurring pattern in the story of the Judges that has been imposed upon it by those known as the Deuteronomic Editors. Their view of Israel's history in this period is therefore presented in a regularly occurring framework that is set around the story of each of the individual Judges. A summary of that framework is given in Judg 2:6–3:6: Israel goes after the alien gods of the Canaanites; God sends punishment upon Israel in the form of an attack from one of the nations that surrounds her; the people repent of their idolatry and cry out to the Lord for deliverance; God heeds their cry and raises up for them a charismatic figure called a Judge, who leads them forth into battle to defeat the enemy. However, the victory is really not won by Israel, but by the Lord who comes to their aid.

Not all of the Judges are military leaders. Shamgar, Tola, Jair, Ibzan, Elon, and Abdon are only briefly mentioned as judging or ruling over the people. Certainly Samson is a unique folk hero, something like a Paul Bunyan of Israel. But the major Judges are endowed with the Spirit of the Lord, which prompts them to call forth the free farmers of the tribes to battle, and to lead them in victory. Indeed, very often, the verb "to judge" (*shapat* in Hebrew) can have the meaning of "to save," and it is the military Judges, inspired by the Spirit of the Lord, who "save" Israel from her attackers with the help of the Lord.

Israel at this time therefore found a source of some unity not only in her common worship of and covenant with one God at one shrine, but also in her common battles against the foreigners who threatened her life. These battles have been named "Holy Wars" by scholars, not because war was so holy, but because the battles were conducted according to strict cultic rules. And it is the Holy War that furnishes the background of Israel's warfare throughout the Book of Judges as well as several centuries after the period of the federation.

In the pattern of the Holy War, when Israel was attacked by some enemy, the Lord raised up a Judge by his Spirit, who

58

called the tribes forth to battle. Not every tribe responded, because they were free farmers who did not want to leave their crops and because often the Judge was totally unknown to them. Nevertheless, those who assembled armed themselves "before the LORD," consecrated their weapons, took vows (cf. Judg 11:30–31)—including the vow to forego sexual intercourse (cf. 2 Sam 11:6–13)—inquired of the Lord (cf. Judg 20:23), and offered a sacrifice to God (cf. 1 Sam 13:8–9). They then marched out to battle with the ark of the covenant going before them as a symbol of the Lord's presence. The number of troops really was not important, however, because it was principally God who fought against the enemy by supernatural means (cf. Judg 7:4–8 and my exposition of Exod 15 in ch. 4). When the victory was won, enemy troops and goods were sacrificed to the Lord in the rite of the ban (see my exposition of Deut 20:10–18 in ch. 8), and the troops were dismissed to return home.

Our text of Judg 4:1–7 has the Holy War as its background, although there are some variations. Deborah is already a Judge and a prophetess when she summons Barak to fight against the Canaanites, who have oppressed Israel for twenty years. Only the troops of the tribes of Naphtali and Zebulun are called out, although this is contradicted by the parallel poetic account in Judg 5. Barak, not Deborah the Judge, leads the battle, and the assurance of victory is given by the prophetic words of Deborah, who also predicts that the Canaanite general, Sisera, will be slain by the hand of a woman (v. 9). But the ark of the covenant goes before the troops, as in the Holy War (v. 14), and it is the Lord who routs the Canaanite troops of Sisera (v. 15).

Forming the Sermon

What are we to make of these battles that we find in the Book of Judges? Certainly they are defensive wars that testify to God's protection of his chosen people, but there is much more to say than that.

First, the question arises as to just why God should protect Israel. They are not a faithful people, as the opening sentence of our text states. "And the people of Israel *again* did what was evil in the sight of the LORD." That is, the Israelites did not keep their covenant with their God, in which they swore to have no other God besides him (Exod 20:3). Repeatedly, they forgot about God's mercies toward them and turned their hearts and their worship to the foreign deities of fertility.

The Israelites were very much like us, you see. They wanted the good things of life, the material comforts, the wine, the grain, the wool, the oil (cf. Hos 2:9, 12). So they turned to the deities whom they thought could furnish them those benefits, just as so many in our day turn to the televangelists or popular writers who promise them success and prosperity and the good life. Indeed, we substitute lots of idols for loyalty to the Lord, don't we?—the job that promises us financial success if we will devote all of our time and energy to it; the lottery or casino or race track where we may strike it rich; the friendship with the important and beautiful people who have it made; the seven-days-a-week, twenty-fours-hour-a-day pursuit of security based on wealth. We, like Israel of old, do not deserve God's protection and redemption of us in Jesus Christ.

Yet, one of the functions of the stories in Judges is to give witness to God's marvelous and merciful patience with his unfaithful people, and that is one of the prominent features of our text. "The people of Israel *again* did what was evil in the sight of the LORD" (v. 1). Over and over again, the Israelites broke their covenant with God. And because God is not mocked, Israel suffered the judgment of God in the form of twenty years of Canaanite domination.

We live in a society that thinks that God never levels his judgments against anybody. But the Scriptures know differently. God subjected his people to oppression at the hands of the Canaanites, and God subjects us to the anxieties, the violence, the sufferings, and the broken relationships that we suffer so often. Our indifference and faithlessness toward our

Lord return in countless tribulations and evil consequences upon our own heads.

And yet—and yet—God willed to save his idolatrous chosen people from their enemies when they cried out for help, and in overflowing mercy and incredible patience he wills to save us from the evil results of our sin also. "While we were yet sinners Christ died for us" (Rom 5:8). God gave his Son to die upon a cross for us, taking all of our sins upon himself, so that when we cry out for succor and rely on the forgiveness of that cross, he counts us righteous in his eyes and does not bring sin's deserved death upon us. For centuries, ever since the time of Israel, God has been forgiving and saving his people in spite of themselves, bringing it all to a glorious climax in that final salvation through Jesus Christ.

Our text sets forth another prominent note, however, and that is the power of God to defeat the forces of evil that threaten our lives. Note the pronouns in v. 7 of the text. Through the words of the prophetess Deborah, God says, "*I* will draw out Sisera, the general of Jabin's army, to meet you by the river Kishon with his chariots and his troops; and *I* will give him into your hand." God has power over the enemy. God could use the Canaanites to punish Israel for her sins, but when Israel implores his salvation, God can also defeat the armies of the Canaanite Sisera, who wishes to destroy Israel. God will not let Israel be destroyed. Sisera may have the horses and chariots against which the peasant Israelites have no chance whatsoever, but they are no match for the Lord. Indeed, in the story that follows, Sisera's powerlessness before the Lord is emphasized by the fact that he flees the battle scene, falls into an exhausted sleep and is killed by the hand of a woman.

Following this is an ancient poem (Judg 5) in which the Canaanite defeat is celebrated and God is pictured as marching to the battle from the southern desert to the Plain of Esdraelon, with the earth trembling and the mountains quaking before him (Judg 5:4–5). And God, who commands the forces of the universe, uses the heavenly hosts ("stars") to fight against Sisera's army (Judg 5:20). It is the Lord who defeats the Canaanites: "The LORD routed Sisera and all his chariots and all his armies before Barak at the edge of the sword" (Judg 4:15).

The God of incredible, patient mercy is also the God of invincible power, who has the might to put his mercy into effect. At the cross on Golgotha, therefore, the Lord chains the forces of evil and death and renders them powerless. Then he rises victorious over sin and death at first light on Easter morn. This God of the Bible punishes us for our unfaithfulness to him, but when we turn to him in trust, he has the power to overcome all our sin, to make of us new persons in Christ, and to grant us eternal life beyond the seeming finality of the grave. In the days of the Judges, God forgave and saved his people. He can do that also in our day if we will trust him with our lives.

❧ 11 ❧

The Rejection of Saul

1 SAMUEL 13:1–15

*P*ERHAPS NO PORTION OF THE OLD TESTAMENT IS MORE important for illustrating the struggles of faith in the real world than are the stories of Saul in 1 Sam 9–31. Here the radical demands of biblical faith confront head-on the complex contingencies of history, to instruct us and to awaken our sympathies. This can all be portrayed when we preach about the rejection of Saul, the first king of Israel.

Plumbing the Text

There are several facts we need to know as background for this story. First, the introduction of a monarchy into Israel's life was made historically necessary by the threat of the Philistines. After that people had come from the island of Crete and settled into five city states along the coast of Palestine, they threatened the twelve-tribe federation of Israel with extinction. For a century, up until about 1020 B.C., the Philistines dominated the Israelites militarily; the loose federation of the Israelites, with its volunteer army of free farmers, was simply too unorganized and spasmodically leaderless to defend itself.

The Israelites therefore pleaded with Samuel to anoint for them a king to lead them in battle (1 Sam 8:19–22). Israel's need for a king introduced a tension into Israel's polity, however, that was never fully overcome, because the real King of Israel was the Lord. Thus, 1 Sam 8:6–7 views the political necessity of the kingship as a faithless rejection of the kingship of God.

Second, after Saul was anointed king (1 Sam 10:1; 11:15), his main task was to defeat the Philistines. His was, first and foremost, a military kingship. (Cf. the summary statement of his battles in 1 Sam 14:47–48, 52.)

Third, we must understand that the battles of Saul and the Israelites against the Philistines and other enemies were conducted according to the ritual rules of the Holy War (see my discussion of Exod 15 in ch. 4). In such warfare, volunteers were summoned from among the free farmers throughout the realm to assemble. The men consecrated themselves and their weapons, took vows,[1] and abstained from normal practices, such as marital intercourse.[2] Before they marched out to battle, a sacrifice was offered by the priest to the Lord, and inquiry was made of God, who replied either that the people would be victorious or that they would be defeated and should not go to battle.[3] The ark of the covenant, symbolizing the presence of God, went before the troops, and it was the Lord who was the principal warrior, with Israel simply aiding him. After the battle was won, all of the enemies and their goods were to be sacrificed to the Lord in what was known as the *herem* or ban, and the troops were dismissed to their homes with the cry, "To your tents, O Israel." It is this pattern of battle that lies behind our text.

Fourth, the final rejection of Saul as king over Israel is recounted in 1 Sam 15, and our text is a prelude to that account. Following closely after the story of the anointing of Saul, 1 Sam 13 sounds the ominous note that Saul's kingship lies under the shadow of God's disapproval from the very beginning.

Forming the Sermon

Saul is obviously a very brave man. In this initial account of his battles with the Philistines, he has three thousand troops gathered about him at Gilgal, but the military supremacy of the enemy is evident. Mustered at Michmash, the Philistines have thirty thousands chariots, each holding two men. Both Michmash and Gilgal are located in the central hill country of Palestine, however, where chariots are largely useless, and the fighting must be done on foot. The intention of the Philistines is apparently just to inspire terror in the Israelite soldiers, a strategy that is quite effective, according to vv. 6–7. Nevertheless, Saul is ready to lead his trembling troops into battle.

The ritual of the Holy War required that a sacrifice be offered to the Lord by the priest, namely by Samuel, before the battle could be joined. Samuel had given Saul strict instructions to wait for him seven days, in order that Samuel might offer burnt offerings and inquire of the Lord (1 Sam 10:8). Saul waited (13:8), but Samuel did not show up. The troops grow restless. They are fearful anyway, and they are all farmers who need to get back to their crops, so they begin silently leaving, one by one. Saul is desperate. He has few enough soldiers as it is, and if some of them desert Saul's situation will be hopeless. In desperation, Saul orders that the burnt offerings be brought to him, and he makes the sacrifice in place of Samuel.

Immediately Samuel appears, and Saul is charged with his sin. "You have not kept the commandment of the LORD your God" (v. 13). Saul has disobeyed the word of the Lord. Whether that refers to the instructions that Samuel gave Saul or to the cultic rules of the Holy War, we are not told. Probably the latter is the case. But it is clear that Saul's sin is disobedience, as it is also in the account of 1 Sam 15, where Saul refuses to carry through the *herem* destruction of the Amalekites, which is demanded by the word of the Lord (Exod 17:14; Deut 25:17–19).[4] His fault is summed up in 1 Sam 15:22: "Behold, to obey is better than sacrifice" (cf. Mark 12:33; Matt 9:13; 12:7). That is, beyond all cultic rules and performances, God desires obedience, and because Saul has not obeyed the word of the Lord, he is not a "man after (God's) own heart," and his kingship is rejected, to be replaced with that of David (1 Sam 13:14).

This account dismays us, doesn't it, because it seems that Saul had no options. Israel was threatened with annihilation at the hands of the Philistines. Saul's troops were deserting. In order to save his people, Saul had to offer that sacrifice and get on with the battle. The historical situation demanded his disobedient action.

Saul is a tragic figure in the Old Testament. His story is the nearest thing we have in Israel to Greek tragedy, for it is the very necessities of his office that lead to Saul's downfall. When we read of his desperation in 1 Sam 28 and of his brave death in 1 Sam 31, our sympathies go out to him.

And Saul's dilemma is not his alone. It is one that is faced by every person who attempts to live a life pleasing to God. It poses the question as to how to be in the world and yet not of it. The Philistines are mustered at Michmash, so what should Saul do? Should he rely on the Word of God and wait, or should he take matters into his own hands and prepare for battle? Apply the question in our own time. Modern Israel is surrounded by Arab nations that are determined to destroy her. What should she do? Should she rely solely on God for her defense, or should she put her trust in a well-trained army? How do we meet the contingencies and ambiguities of history and yet put our whole trust in the Lord our God?

I remember so well during the Second World War how many young pacifist men struggled with that question. Adolph Hitler's *Blitzkrieg* was swallowing up Europe, and the United States had enlisted its young men in the military draft. But some of those drafted were committed Christians who believed it was wrong to go to war. Yet Hitler could be stopped only by military means; all negotiations such as those of Neville Chamberlain had failed. So what were those young pacifist men to do? Should they have denied their faith and gone to fight, or should they go to jail for their refusal? Hundreds of them had to make that difficult decision.

Our Lord presses the decision hard upon us: "Sell what you have, and give to the poor . . . and come, follow me" (Mark 10:21); "No one who puts his hand to the plow and looks back is fit for the kingdom of God" (Luke 9:62); "He who loves father or mother more than me is not worthy of me" (Matt 10:37). And we reply, "Lord, we have responsibilities in this world, that you yourself have laid upon us. How can we possibly neglect those to give up everything and follow you?"

When my husband and I taught at a seminary in Pennsylvania, there showed up at the registrar's office one day a fellow from India, who wanted to enroll in the three-year course. We duly admitted him, but then we found out that he had a wife and four children at home in India. "Who is caring for them?" we asked him. "The Lord will provide," he replied.

The Lord will provide. Will he? Will he defeat the Philistines who batter at our gates? Will he defeat a monster who is killing millions in Europe? Will he provide for our loved ones if we desert them to follow what we think is Jesus' way? How do you live in the world, with all of its demands and necessities, and yet perfectly obey the word of the Lord, who asks our sole loyalty? How can we be in the world and yet not of it?

If we truly want to live Christian lives, in obedience to our Lord, we have to wrestle with those questions daily, in every decision we make. And because that is true, perhaps two things need to be said.

First, it is not easy to be a faithful Christian. There are preachers who glibly assure us that it is very easy to be good, if we will only agree with them and do what they tell us. But the biblical Christian faith brings with it a radical demand for sole loyalty to God, that makes it always necessary to decide how to live out that loyalty in the real world. And that decision is not easy. There is nothing simple about piety.

Second, because as Christians we all have to wrestle with the commandments of God, perhaps that wrestling can also teach all of us a little more understanding and sympathy with our fellow Christians. Those of us who were gung ho to defeat Hitler in the Second World War looked down with a certain amount of scorn on our pacifist young men who went to prison for their belief. But they were attempting to be faithful to their God, as does every sincere Christian. And where we disagree on a course of action—if true faithfulness be the criterion—we should honor the faith that is nevertheless being expressed in the course we would not have chosen. Living the Christian life is not easy. We all struggle together to live it. And we need to count as beloved brothers and sisters those who struggle with us.

Notes

1. Cf. the story of Jephthah, Judg 11.
2. Cf. the story of Uriah and David, 2 Sam 11.
3. Cf. "the LORD has given *so and so* into your hands," Judg 3:28; 4:7, 14; 7:9, 15; 18:10; 20:28, et al.
4. Saul pleads in 1 Sam 15:21 that it was the people who were disobedient and that they saved the best animals of the Amalekites, because they intended to offer them as a sacrifice to the Lord. A sacrifice is different from the ban, however.

᪻ 12 ᪻

Uzzah and the Ark

2 SAMUEL 6:1–15

*K*ARL BARTH USED TO SPEAK OF THE "STRANGE, NEW world of the Bible." The account of Uzzah and the ark in this passage bespeaks that strangeness, because it deals with the power of holiness, an understanding of which has almost totally dropped out of our culture. The story concerns King David's attempt to bring the Ark of the Covenant into Jerusalem.

Plumbing the Text

The only description of the Ark of the Covenant that we have comes from the Priestly Writers, who tell us that God commanded Israel at Mt. Sinai to build a tabernacle and an ark. There is no reason, however, to doubt the priestly description of the ark given in Exod 25:10–22.

The ark was a portable shrine in the form of a rectangular box made of acacia wood overlaid with gold. On each side of the ark were poles inserted through rings, enabling the ark to be carried. On top of the ark was a slab of gold called the mercy seat, and at each end of the mercy seat there was a golden cherub that had outspread wings and that faced the mercy seat. Most important was the fact that the ark was considered to be the base of the throne of God, who was invisibly enthroned above the cherubim (1 Sam 4:4). Therefore, where the ark was, God was present.[1]

The Ark of the Covenant was the central cult object in Israel for hundreds of years. It led the people through their wilderness wanderings (Num 22:33–35), accompanied their entrance into the promised land (Josh 4), went with the Israelite troops into battle (e.g., at Jericho, Josh 6), and was housed in a tent at the central shrine of the tribal federation, first at Shechem, then perhaps at Gilgal, and finally at Shiloh, in the time of the Judges and Samuel (1 Sam 3).

In the stories leading up to our text, 1 Sam 4 tells us that the ark was captured in a battle with the Philistines, a terrible blow to Israel (cf. 1 Sam 4:17–22). The presence of the ark brought nothing but disaster to the Philistines, however, and they moved it from city to city in a vain attempt to escape its terrible effects (1 Sam 5). Finally, they put it on a driverless cart and sent it back to Beth-Shemesh in Israel. But the inhabitants of that city could not handle its power either, and finally, the ark was placed in the house of Abin'adab in Kiriath-jearim (or Baal-judah, 2 Sam 6:2), where it bestowed abundant blessings for twenty years.

David learned of the well-being of Abin'adab and determined to bring the ark to his new capitol city of Jerusalem. According to our text, the ark was placed on a new cart for the journey. When the cart came to the threshing floor of Nacon, the oxen pulling the cart stumbled, and Uzzah put out his hand to steady the ark, lest it tumble from the cart. Uzzah was immediately struck dead, a result that angered David. But having witnessed the power of the ark's presence, David feared to bring it into Jerusalem. Instead the ark was deposited in the house of Obed-edom the Gittite. But Obed-edom too was blessed by the ark's presence, and so David brought the ark into Jerusalem, with the king and the inhabitants of Jerusalem dancing and singing in wild exuberance before it.

Forming the Sermon

Most modern congregations are dismayed by this story of the death of Uzzah. After all, the man just wanted to make sure that the Ark of the Covenant did not fall off of the cart that was carrying it. His was an act of concern for the ark. Should he then die for such a good act?

That which we moderns do not understand is the power associated with divine holiness. Every religion has some sense of the holy. It is a primal phenomenon that is not limited to biblical religion, and it manifests itself in the experience of power that does not belong to the profane, everyday realm, but that has the quality of total otherness.

In his famous book, *The Idea of the Holy*, Rudolf Otto has described the holy as the *mysterium tremendum*, as that which is an undefined and uncanny energy, imponderable, incomprehensible, always something more than the ordinary, both fascinating and fearful, that repels human beings from it and yet draws them to it.[2]

The holy can have the appearance of simply impersonal power. For example, the Priestly Writers tell us in Exod 29:37 that whoever touches the holy altar becomes holy. In Num 4:20, whoever gazes on the holy things becomes holy, or in Ezek 44:19, whoever touches the garments of the priests has holiness communicated to him or her. The same is true in the New Testament. When the woman who has had a flow of blood for twelve years touches the fringe of Jesus' garment, Luke tells us that she is immediately healed and Jesus says, "Some one touched me; for I perceive that power has gone forth from me" (Luke 8:46).

Holiness is power. As a result, all religions set up rules and rituals for their worship that keep the sphere of the holy from being mixed with the profane (cf. Exod 19:12). The purpose is not only to prevent the holy from being contaminated but also to protect the worshipers from the power of the holy that can break out upon them.

Most frequently in the Scriptures, holiness is connected with God. "Holy, holy, holy," sing the seraphim in Isaiah's vision (Isa 6:3). Above all else, God is holy. His holiness is synonymous with his divinity, distinguishing him from all other things, persons, and places, so that he can be described as the Wholly Other, qualitatively different from everything and everyone in creation. That is not a static quality, however,

71

but a power, activity, energy, vitality beyond all human imagining. The God of the Bible is always on the move toward his
goal, always active, always working his effects upon his world,
and so he is properly described in the Bible by what he does.
As some have said, "God" is not a noun but a verb.

The holy God takes things, persons, and places into his
realm and reserves them for his purpose, so that they become
holy, set apart for God's use, as with the holy things in the
temple and the priests' garments in the references given
above. Indeed, God even does that with times. The Gospel
according to John repeatedly tells us that Jesus uses certain
times to "manifest his glory," his otherness, his holiness, and
the events that take place in those times are considered by
us to be "miracles," strange, extraordinary happenings for
which we cannot account.

In our text, the Ark of the Covenant is the base of the
invisible Lord's throne. God is present, enthroned above it.
Thus the ark is surrounded by holiness, concentrating the
power of God about it. And the holy God needs no human
help to prevent the ark from tumbling! Uzzah has treated the
ark like any ordinary box, much like we consider our worship
ordinary. But the ark is not ordinary. It belongs to God's realm,
and it needs no help to keep it steady. Throughout the stories
of the ark in 1 Sam 4 through 2 Sam 6, the ark has brought
both blessing and ill to its keepers. God determines what the
ark does, not human beings. God is in charge.

We modern worshipers think to be very familiar with God.
We enter into his worship sometimes very casually, often thinking about something else. We act as if his commands are only
suggestions. And like Eve conversing with the serpent in the
Garden of Eden, we talk *about* God. We discuss him as an object
"out there." We decide whether we can trust him or not, and
we make him an object of speculation. These days, we even
give him new names to express our familiarity with him—
Friend, Mother, Lover—and we let our imaginations run wild
to shape him to accord with our human experiences. As a result,
this story of Uzzah in 2 Samuel offends our sensibilities. What
kind of God is this whose holiness strikes a man dead?

72

The God of Uzzah's story and of all the Scriptures is a
God of holy power, totally overwhelming in his difference
from us sinful creatures. And he can, indeed, kill or make
alive.

> See now that I, even I, am he,
>   and there is no god beside me;
> I kill and I make alive;
>   I wound and I heal;
>   and there is none that can deliver
>   out of my hand. (Deut 32:39)

We do well to approach such a God in fear and trembling
therefore. The worshipers of the Old Testament knew that.
"Put off your shoes," Moses was commanded from that burning bush, "for the place on which you are standing is holy
ground" (Exod 3:5). "Behold, I have taken upon myself to
speak to the LORD," Abraham uttered, "I who am but dust
and ashes" (Gen 18:27). "Woe is me," Isaiah cried out, "For I
am lost! . . . for my eyes have seen the King, the LORD of
hosts" (Isa 6:5). "Depart from me," Peter begged of Jesus,
"for I am a sinful man, O Lord" (Luke 5:8). Sin cannot live
before the holiness that is pure and unsullied in its perfec-
tion. We creatures, corrupted by our sin, have no right to
stand before a God who is pure and righteous, and we should
never think that he cannot do without us. It is only by his
grace that he lets us live at all.

But grace he extends to us, good Christians, the grace of
love and acceptance and solicitude. Whenever he confronts
the sinful mortals of the Bible, his first word is, "Fear not!"
"Fear not," he says to Abraham, "I am your shield" (Gen 15:1).
"Fear not, for I am with you," he assures the exiles in a foreign
land (Isa 43:5). "Fear not, little flock, for it is your Father's
good pleasure to give you the kingdom" (Luke 12:32). "Fear
not, I am the first and the last, and the living one," says our
Lord Christ. "I died, and behold I am alive forevermore, and
I have the keys of Death and Hades" (Rev 1:17).

God, the holy Lord of life and death, has willed that we
have life, and his risen Son holds the keys of life abundant
and eternal. So, yes, we approach him in fear and trembling,

always reverent and bowing before his holiness. But we also approach him in confidence through Jesus Christ, and find his help in the time of our need (cf. Heb 4:14–16).

Notes

1. The Deuteronomic Writers somewhat demythologize the understanding of the ark. Their view is that God is enthroned in heaven and the ark is simply the container for the tablets of the law. See Gerhard Von Rad, *Old Testament Theology* (trans. D. M. G. Stalker; Edinburgh: Oliver & Boyd, 1962), 1:238.

2. *The Idea of the Holy: An Inquiry into the Non-Rational Factor in the Idea of the Divine and Its Relation to the Rational* (rev. ed.; trans. J. W. Harvey; London: Oxford University Press, 1946), cited in J. Muilenburg, "Holiness," *Interpreter's Dictionary of the Bible* (ed. G. A. Buttrick; 4 vols. and suppl.; Nashville: Abingdon, 1962–1976), 2:616.

❧ 13 ❧

The Translation of Elijah

2 KINGS 2:1–12

*T*HERE ARE SOME PASSAGES IN THE OLD TESTAMENT THAT we simply do not understand. This is the stated Old Testament lesson for Transfiguration Sunday, the Sunday before Ash Wednesday, in Cycle B of the three-year lectionary. But when the passage is read before a congregation, usually neither pastor nor people know what to make of it. The passage is difficult for us because its meaning seems to be so opaque. Certainly it is an appropriate reading for Transfiguration Sunday, however, as I hope to make clear.

Plumbing the Text

These verses begin what is known as the cycle of Elisha stories that are gathered together in 1 Kgs 2:1–13:21. Actually, our text forms one unit with the whole of 1 Kgs 2, but the meaning can become clear from the first twelve verses.

We know from v. 1 in the text that Elijah's ministry is about to end with his "translation" or ascent into heaven in a whirlwind. He will not undergo death, but will be transported immediately to the heavenly realm, reminding us of the notice about Enoch in Gen 5:24 and of the ascension of our Lord.

With this first verse we have entered the realm of mystery, having to do with events that are not of this earth, as the transfiguration of Christ was not of this earth (Mark 9:2–8). So the two texts go well together.

Elijah and Elisha go on their way together in a rather pointless journey, from Gilgal to Bethel to Jericho (which is only a few miles from Gilgal) to the Jordan. All of the towns named are located in the hill country of Benjamin, and there is no notice given as to why Elijah leads his apprentice from one place to the next. At each site mentioned, Elijah tries to rid himself of the company of Elisha, but the latter shows his absolute loyalty to his master by refusing to stay behind, sealing his determination with the phrase, "As the LORD lives." Nothing stronger can be said, because the Lord is the supremely living One.

At each place, the two are also met by "sons of the prophets." That is a designation for the early, non-writing prophets, who usually lived together as bands of prophets in closed colonies at the various sanctuaries. They had two characteristics that distinguished them from the later writing prophets. First, revelation was given to them through the Spirit, whereas the emphasis in the prophetic writings is on revelation by the word of the Lord. Second, most of them were ecstatic prophets, who by the gift of the Spirit were given heightened physical and mental powers in a state of ecstasy (cf. 1 Sam 10:11–12). For example, in the Spirit, Elijah was able to run ahead of the chariot of Ahab the seventeen miles from the top of Mt. Carmel to the plain of Jezreel (1 Kgs 18:46). Similarly, by the power of the Spirit, these early prophets could speak the words of the Lord that gave meaning and hope to the present and the future. It was only later when they corrupted their prophetic office, by pridefully speaking their own words and not God's, that they were condemned by many of the writing prophets.

The fact that these sons of the prophets are true prophets is confirmed in our text by their foreknowledge of Elijah's departure. They are, however, forbidden to speak further of the matter.

Elijah's power as a prophet is attested in this particular story by his parting of the waters of the Jordan, reminiscent of Moses, the greatest of the prophets, at the Reed Sea (Exod 14:21, 27) and of God's act for Joshua at the entrance into the promised land (Josh 3:14–17).

Before his translation into heaven, Elijah grants Elisha one request, and Elisha asks for a double share of Elijah's prophetic spirit. Elisha is not trying to be greater than his master. Rather, he is asking for the inheritance that was given a first-born son by his father (Deut 21:17). Thus, we are enabled to know that Elisha is Elijah's successor, inheriting Elijah's prophetic spirit, in an intimate relation likened to that of a father with his son (cf. v. 12). Elisha will be confirmed as the successor, however, only if he witnesses that which ordinary sight cannot see—the translation of Elijah into heaven by the whirlwind (v. 10).

Further, as Elijah's successor, Elisha is called to complete Elijah's task of toppling the great Omri dynasty in the northern kingdom and of putting Jehu on the throne of Israel and Hazael on the throne of Syria. In short, Elisha is called to complete the work of the prophetic revolution, which God had foretold (1 Kgs 19:15–18).

As the two men talk and walk on together, they are separated by a chariot of fire and horses of fire, and at that moment, Elijah is taken up, not in the chariot, as artists and tradition have long portrayed, but by the whirlwind. Overcome by the vision, Elisha cries out to his father-master that he sees the chariots and horsemen of Israel.

Who are these strange chariots and horses or horsemen? In other passages of the Old Testament, similar images represent the power and presence of God. Fire is frequently associated with the theophany or appearance of the Lord (Exod 3:2; 24:17, numerous passages), and the horses and chariots are symbols of his unseen power (2 Kgs 6:15–18; 7:6–7). Connected with Elijah, therefore, are the power and presence of God, and both are concentrated in the Word of God that the prophet speaks. That word is Israel's defense. Elijah, in the power of the Spirit, spoke the word that overcame Israel's enemies, and that word and Spirit are now to be passed on to Elisha.

The real point of the passage and of the chapter as a whole is contained in the following v. 15: "The spirit of Elijah rests on Elisha," and the miracles of Elisha that follow in the Elisha cycle are intended as testimony to that gift. Since, however, this passage is linked to the account of the Transfiguration, we will consider another preaching approach.

Forming the Sermon

We enter onto another plane of reality in this text, as is also the case with the transfiguration of our Lord. In the latter text, heaven is the setting of the story, and God's glory illumines every detail. The high mount of transfiguration is the place of divine revelation. Jesus' robes shine glistening white, whiter than any earthly fuller could bleach them. There is the voice of God speaking from the cloud to the three terrified disciples, and the time of the story is the time of the end, when human history has been brought to its conclusion. The action takes place on the seventh day, when God has completed his work. And Jesus is seen talking to Moses and Elijah, that is, the sacred history has been fulfilled. In short, human time has fallen from view, and we are allowed a glimpse of the eternal realm of heaven.

So too in this story of the finale of Elijah's ministry. The human earthly sphere is being gradually left behind, and we are being drawn into the heavenly realm, a reality that human eyes cannot see but that is granted only to faith.

It has often been said that when persons are about to die, they gradually withdraw from their loved ones and surroundings, as if they are entering a different realm. That is what is happening here in our text. Elijah will not experience death, but he gradually withdraws from earth. He makes three attempts to get rid of Elisha and to be by himself, but Elisha's faithfulness finally convinces him that Elisha must share in the experience of Elijah's departure.

The sons of the prophets know what is going to happen, but they are not allowed to enter into the event. Instead fifty of them stand "at some distance" (v. 7) and can only observe from afar that Elijah and Elisha have somehow crossed the Jordan and that Elijah suddenly disappears from their sight. They do not see the chariots of Israel and its horsemen. That vision is granted only to Elisha's eyes of faith. Their distance from the event is further emphasized by the fact that after Elijah's departure, Elisha suddenly stands in their midst (v. 15)—they do not know how. And they think that perhaps Elijah has just been transported by the Spirit to some other place (vv. 16–18).

Everything is mysterious, incomprehensible to human eyes and mind, revelatory of another realm of reality that human beings cannot see or experience by themselves, but that can only be granted by God.

In other words, what our text is revealing to us is that there is another reality beyond our earthly existence, a realm of God, of heaven, if you will, that lies beyond our senses and experience, but that is absolutely real. Moreover, that realm in which God dwells and to which the faithful are transported, is a place of power. It is the realm of God from which come the chariots and horsemen of the Lord, those heavenly powers by which God guards and defends his people.

Most important, those heavenly powers from God are concentrated in his word. They were concentrated in the words and works of Elijah and Elisha that toppled a dynasty and brought the dead to life again (2 Kgs 4:32–37). Supremely, they were concentrated in the Word made flesh, Jesus Christ, whom all the evil of human beings and death itself could not defeat.

By the power of his Word, who is Jesus Christ, God works in this ordinary world of ours, hidden, unseen, unknown except to those who have the eyes of faith and who listen to hear his speaking. By that powerful Word, God is working out his purpose for human life. By the might that is the Son of God, he is bringing that purpose to fulfillment, until all of faith are brought into his realm, and God is all in all.

❧ 14 ❧

Put Away Your
Foreign Wives and Children

EZRA 9–10

WHILE IT IS DOUBTFUL THAT MANY PREACHERS HAVE based sermons on these two chapters in the post-exilic Book of Ezra, they do have surprising relevance for our lives today. They therefore perhaps deserve our more careful attention.

Plumbing the Text

From the time of her entrance into the land of Canaan and throughout the following centuries of her existence, Old Testament Israel was forbidden intermarriage and cultural assimilation to the original inhabitants of the promised land. The ancient Holiness Code of Leviticus forbids Israel to "do as they do in the land of Canaan" (Lev 18:1–4), and an even older Ritual Decalogue of Exod 34:11–16 forbids worship of Canaanite deities and intermarriage with Canaanite women (cf. Deut 7:3–5). Centuries later, the fifth century B.C. prophecies of Malachi condemn those who have divorced the wives of their youth to marry non-Israelite women (Mal 2:10–16).

The reason for the prohibition is very clear. The Canaanites were worshipers of pagan fertility gods and goddesses, whose rituals included cult prostitution and even child sacri-

fice (cf. e.g., 1 Kgs 14:21–24; Deut 18:9–14), and such religion had no place in the worship of the Lord God of Israel.
Israel's Lord had delivered her out of bondage in Egypt, and
Israel's grateful response to his grace was to have no other
gods besides him (Exod 20:3), to follow only his covenant
commandments (Lev 18:4–5), and to order her community
according to the Lord's will and mercy.

All of that tradition enters into Ezra's prayer in Ezra
9:6–15, which rehearses Israel's sinful past. Far from being a
community that cleaved only to the Lord, Israel repeatedly
went after the Baal gods and goddesses of the Canaanites,
took upon herself pagan ways of the foreign nations, and
forgot the One who redeemed her out of slavery. As a result,
Israel's Lord delivered her into foreign exile. But now, in
Ezra's time, God has shown favor to his people once more, by
allowing a remnant to return to Palestine, according to the
decree of Cyrus of Persia. Ezra's community is a tiny little
subprovince of the Persian Empire ("bondmen," 9:9). Nevertheless they have had the freedom to reconstruct Jerusalem
under Nehemiah, to reestablish the temple and its worship
under Zerubbabel and Joshua the high priest, and now, under
Ezra, to reconstitute their religious community.

Yet, the Israelites have not learned a thing. Ezra is told by
the officials that some of their Zadokite priests, Levites, and
upper-class laity have married non-Israelite women and have
had children by them. "The holy race has mixed itself with the
peoples of the land" (9:2). Far from being a people separated
to the service of the Lord (which is the meaning of "holy
race"), a number have adopted Canaanite customs and worship, or at least are in danger of doing so in their households.

Apparently the number of those who married Canaanite
women was small, some twenty-seven members of the high
priest's family, and eighty-six laity, out of a population of
about fifty thousand. Yet these were community leaders,
including Jeshua, the son of the high priest Jozadak (10:18),
and all had a great deal of influence among the returnees.

Ezra is appalled and enters into rites connected with
fasting and mourning. His concern is not for racial purity, but

for religious purity in the sight of God. His community is a fragile little remnant that for a brief moment lives in God's favor. But if the community is drawn away to worship other deities, then Ezra fears that once again Israel will be sent into exile and indeed, totally disappear from history. In Ezra's eyes, the actual existence of the post-exilic community is at stake.

The result is that at the suggestion of one Shecaniah, Ezra calls a community-wide assembly to meet at Jerusalem in three days (10:7–8). Huddled together on the square in front of the temple in the cold December rain, the men of Israel repent of their assimilation and marriages with Canaanite women, offer guilt offerings, and enter into a covenant to "put away" their foreign wives and children. Only three persons oppose the move (10:15). But because the matter takes time, a commission is appointed to meet with those who have intermarried, and after three months, the separation is complete. Israel's community is once again a people "not reckoning itself among the nations" (Num 23:9).

Forming the Sermon

Put away your foreign wives and children! For us that is a terrible command, especially when it is attributed to the God who says, in Malachi, "I hate divorce" (Mal 2:16), and whose Son has taught, "What . . . God has joined together, let not man put asunder" (Mark 10:9–10). We are most likely to doubt that God ever willed such a move on Ezra's part, and we would much prefer to attribute such exclusivism to ancient pride and racial hatred. Rather than excluding others, we believe we should find all persons acceptable.

Certainly divorcing foreign wives and sending them away with their children would cause untold suffering. No mention is made in our text about any care that was provided for them. Probably the divorced women returned to their parents' homes, because single women in Israel had no means of support or protection unless those were furnished by the society. Certainly we must assume, too, that there were some

82

bonds of affection between the husbands and the banished wives and children, and the severance of those bonds must have caused sorrow and pain. The whole thing sounds reprehensible to us.

There is a good deal more at stake here than our first reactions would recognize, however. We could put it in the form of questions: Should the biblical faith be preserved? Would it matter if Judaism disappeared? Or closer to home, would it matter if the Christian faith ceased to exist?

To be sure, we could make up our own religion—and a lot of people are doing that these days. But does a self-made faith convey to us the forgiveness of God for all of the wrong we have done, or his comfort and guidance in times of distress, or his assurance to us of eternal life after death? We can not easily manufacture those gifts for ourselves. The biblical faith conveys to us grace that we never can know from any other source than from our heavenly Father.

Surprisingly enough, then, whom we marry has an influence on whether or not we and our communities remain committed to our Christian faith. Every religion has a set of doctrines or beliefs, a manner of worship, and an ethic that is practiced. And lying behind all of those in the biblical faith is a history of what God has said and done through four thousand years up to the present. Those who are Christians, then, have particular beliefs about the nature and activity of God through the centuries; they worship in particular ways that include sacraments, and they attempt to follow particular ethical norms in their individual and communal daily lives.

Picture, however, a Christian who marries someone who believes none of those things about God, or who has other very contrary ideas about God's nature; who never engages in Christian worship practices or goes to church; who views a Christian lifestyle as foolishness in a society where material success is the goal of life. After a while, the Christian spouse may be influenced to forget all about his or her Christian beliefs, to neglect Christian worship, and to conduct everyday life according to society's standards. Similarly, the children may not be taught the faith. The family's faith can be lost. And if that happens to a number of families in a community, after a while Christian faith and practice can disappear in that society.

The apostle Paul was quite aware of this danger. The churches that he founded were tiny little communities holding on to their faith in the midst of a pagan Roman world. And so to the church in Corinth, Paul wrote, "Do not be mismated with unbelievers. . . . what has a believer in common with an unbeliever?" (2 Cor 6:14, 15). Paul knew that a new and struggling faith-community could be swallowed up by the pagan society around it.

Similarly, still today Orthodox, Conservative, and Reformed Jews are all seriously concerned that Judaism is being threatened with extinction by intermarriage with non-Jews. Writes Dow Marmur, ". . . the greatest danger to Jewish survival outside Israel today is not anti-Semitism but assimilation, epitomized by the threat of intermarriage . . . [it] is a direct threat to Judaism, for without Jews, Judaism cannot exist."[1] Such was the same threat that led Ezra to demand that foreign wives and children be put away from the struggling post-exilic Jewish Palestinian community of the fourth century.

I personally have encountered the pain that Paul's command in 2 Cor 6 can cause Christian believers, however, and that must have been present in Ezra's community. When I was speaking about marriage at a women's college some years ago, a young women came to me, sobbing with grief. She had recently joined a Christian fundamentalist campus group, and they had insisted that she break off her engagement to a young male student who was not a believer. She had obeyed the stricture, but it had devastated her. She was unable to study, to eat, or to function and was obviously consumed with grief over her lost love for her fiance.

What the fundamentalist campus group had overlooked was another of Paul's teachings in 1 Cor 7:12–14:

> To the rest I say, not the Lord, that if any brother has a wife who is an unbeliever, and she consents to live with him, he should not divorce her. If any woman has a husband who is an

unbeliever, and he consents to live with her, she should not divorce him. For the unbelieving husband is consecrated through his wife, and the unbelieving wife is consecrated through her husband. Otherwise, your children would be unclean, but as it is they are holy.

Paul does not counsel divorce, as did Ezra. Rather, his hope is that the faith of the believer will be so solid, so firm, that it will influence and sanctify the whole family.

Surely such is often the case. I know several families in which the manner of life of a believing and loving wife has so impressed a husband that he has eventually joined the church himself and become a Christian. And certainly a husband firm in his Christian faith could have the same effect on an unbelieving wife. Christians who practice their faith can have a transforming effect on their families and children and on the communities around them.

So the lesson from Ezra is clear: We should be aware of the danger with which marriage with unbelievers may threaten a home and a community. Easy accommodation to unbelief can destroy the Christian faith, as it threatened to destroy post-exilic Judaism, and as it still threatens Judaism and Christianity today. If at all possible, Christians should marry Christians. But where a believer is mated with an unbeliever, then the Christian mate bears the responsibility so to live a Christian life of love every day that home and community are sanctified by that love and faith and are themselves gradually drawn to confess Jesus Christ.

Notes

1. *Intermarriage* (London: Reform Synagogues of Great Britain, 1978), 2.

❧ 15 ❧

The Persecution of the Jews

ESTHER 7:1–6, 9–10; 9:20–22

*T*HESE ARE THE STATED OLD TESTAMENT TEXTS FOR THE twenty-sixth Sunday in Pentecost or Ordinary Time in Cycle B of the three-year lectionary. As such they are appropriately paired with Mark 9:38–50 and Ps 124. (Jas 5:13–20 is the epistle lesson.) The use of these Esther texts furnishes the preacher with a golden opportunity to deal with anti-Semitism.

Plumbing the Texts

The Book of Esther is a combination of fact and fiction. King Ahasuerus in the book is the historical Persian ruler Xerxes (486–465 B.C.), who in fact ruled over an empire stretching from India to Ethiopia (1:1). The mentions of the superb postal system (3:13; 8:10), the keeping of an official diary (2:23; 6:1–2), and the form of execution all accord with Persian history. But these have been used to tell a story that is a superb piece of fictional writing, full of vivid characterizations, plots and counter-plots, tensions and their denouments. Probably the book was written during the time of heavy oppression of the Jews in the Hellenic empire of the second century B.C.

The book found its place in the canon as the explanation of the Jewish Feast of Purim, the name that comes from the wicked Haman's casting of the lot, or Pur, to single out Jews for execution (3:7; 9:26–28). Purim is a minor Jewish festival dedicated to revelry, feasting, the exchange of gifts of food, and the reading of the Book of Esther in the synagogue. It is not a religious festival, and the Book of Esther is not an openly religious book. God is never mentioned in the tale. Esther gains the crown as queen, simply because she is picked out of the king's harem as being especially beautiful and lovely. And it is her decree that leads to the slaying of Haman and his ten sons, as well as seventy-five thousand enemies of the Jews—hardly biblically ethical according to most of the Bible's standards of morality.

The stated texts from Esther cannot really be understood unless the preacher briefly tells the story of the entire book. Thus a reading of Esther's nine chapters is almost mandatory for the preacher before preparing the sermon.

Forming the Sermon

Throughout their history, Israel and the Jews have suffered persecution. Clearest in our memory of course is the holocaust under Hitler in Nazi Germany during the Second World War, when Hitler ordered the systematic gassing of six million Jews, along with countless gypsies and handicapped people and others deemed unworthy of life. Today, there are still Arabs in the Middle East who want to eliminate the modern state of Israel. And not too long ago in this country, a Jew was unacceptable in some country clubs and hotels and businesses.

The question arises, therefore, as to why the Jews have always been persecuted. Many supposed Christians have attributed their hatred of the Jews to the fact that the Jews were enemies of Christ, and they have called the Jews Christ-slayers, despite the fact that our Lord himself and his disciples were Jews. Others have hated the Jews because they envy the accomplishments and financial success of some of them.

But the Book of Esther digs deeper than that as it portrays the character of Haman, the king's prime minister.

Haman tells King Ahasuerus, the Jews' "laws are different from those of every other people, and they do not keep the king's laws, so that it is not for the king's profit to tolerate them . . . let it be decreed that they be destroyed" (3:8–9). The Jews are "different," and that Haman cannot tolerate.

More than that, Haman hates the Jews and the Jewish man Mordecai, the uncle and guardian of Esther, because Mordecai will not bow down to him (3:1–3). Haman is a very important figure in his own self-estimation. In fact his ego is enormous. "Whom would the king delight to honor more than me?" he proudly asserts to himself (6:6). "What does this little scum Mordecai mean by not paying me obeisance? He's only a Jew. And by heaven, I'll have him hanged."

The figures of the Jews in the Book of Esther are by no means inferior, however. Mordecai, simply out of kindness, warns the king through Esther, of a plot to kill the king (2:22–23). Esther risks her life by approaching the king's court when she has not been called. "If I perish, I perish," she says (4:16). And despite her high position and her absorption into the Persian court and ways, she will not forget her kindred Jews throughout the empire or give up her own Jewish identity (8:6).

But the Jews are "different." There is no doubt about that. As Balaam said many centuries before, Israel of the Old Testament is "a people dwelling alone, and not reckoning itself among the nations" (Num 23:9). It is not like the other peoples and nations of the ancient Near East. It does not have natural ties among its people of blood or soil or background or status. It is a "mixed multitude," as Exodus records (12:38). That which binds the Israelites of the Old Testament together as a people is their common redemption out of slavery in Egypt and their common entrance into a covenant with their Lord. "If you will obey my voice and keep my covenant, you shall be my own possession among all peoples; for the earth is mine, and you shall be to me a kingdom of priests and a holy nation" (Exod 19:5–6). Such were the words that God spoke to the Israelites through Moses at Mt. Sinai in the thirteenth century B.C. The Israelites of the Old Testament

88

and those Jewish descendants who are faithful to the covenant today were chosen by God to be his special people. They are a holy nation, which means they are set apart for God's purpose. And they are a kingdom of priests, which means that they are the ones who mediate the knowledge of God to all the world, as God's witnesses.

How that does rile some people today! Like Haman, they simply cannot stand the thought that the Jews are special people, and especially that they are chosen by God. Hitler and some biblical theologians in the Third Reich abandoned such teachings of the Old Testament. But unless we understand God's choice of Israel, we cannot understand any portion of the Bible, including the New Testament.

According to the Scriptures, Israel is not made God's elected people for privilege. Israel is chosen for *service* to God. "To me the people of Israel are servants whom I brought forth out of the land of Egypt," God declares (Lev 25:55). Throughout the Old Testament, Israel testifies to what that servitude has cost her (cf. e.g., Jacob's/Israel's wounding in Gen 32:25–32). When I had a conversation with a Jewish woman some time ago, she remarked, "I don't want to be a member of God's chosen people; I just want to be like everyone else." Service to the Lord of the universe is costly. It means that Israel cannot follow the ways and worship and laws of the peoples around her (Esth 3:8; cf. Lev 18:1–4). It means that she has to obey God's commandments in all areas of her life, and worship him alone. It means that she is never her own, self-ruled and independent, but that she is always inextricably tied to God's will and God's purpose. If she strays from those, she becomes "No people" (Hos 1:9), without identity and without purpose, subject to the judgment of God.

But God chose Israel and set his love upon her, because God loves all people. The Bible tells us that God made the world very good, but that we corrupted every part of God's creation with our sin—with our attempts to be our own gods and goddesses. Consequently we brought upon ourselves and all people the curse of broken community, corrupted relationships, toilsome labor, a ravished nature, and finally death (Gen 3–11). God would not give up on us, however. Instead he called Abraham and his family out of Mesopotamia in the eighteenth century B.C. to be the beginning of a new people. And through that people, God promised that he would reverse the effects of our cursed rebellion and bring blessing on all the families of the earth, restoring his creation to the goodness that he intended for it in the beginning (Gen 12:1–3). God chose Abraham and his descendants in Israel, because he loves us all and wants to give all of us abundant life.

To be sure, God works in the lives and affairs of all peoples. The Old Testament is very clear about that (cf. e.g., Amos 9:7). But how do we know that? How do we know that God loves all people? Through the Old Testament's witness of Israel and supremely through the New Testament's witness to Jesus Christ, a descendant of Abraham and of David (Matt 1:1). Israel and her descendants were chosen as the medium God uses to bring blessing on us all. But as the Book of Esther and history tell us, throughout their existence as a people the Jews have suffered for being chosen and different.

The Apostle Paul tells us, however, that you and I and all Christians have been grafted into the root of Israel (Rom 11:17–24). Or in Ephesians, it is said that we have joined the covenant community of Israel (2:11–18), to become the new Israel of God in Jesus Christ (Gal 6:16). We have been given the same service that Israel in the Old Testament was given—to be a holy nation, set apart for God's purpose, as a kingdom of priests, to be the witnesses of God's marvelous deeds in the world (1 Pet 2:9–10). We stand under the same commandments that Israel knew, therefore, to worship our one God alone, and to love him with all of our hearts and minds and strength (Exod 20:3; Deut 6:5; Mark 12:30).

Although the good news of Jesus Christ has been entrusted to us instead of to the Jews, who have rejected it for a time, Paul further tells us that God has used that rejection to give us Gentiles time to come into the covenant community. But God has not rejected his people, and in the end, faithful Israel too will be saved (Rom 11). God chose Israel, and now he has chosen us as members of his covenant people, in order to bring his blessing on the world for which he gave his only begotten Son.

To hate the Jews, therefore, and to persecute them, as they are persecuted in the time of Esther, is to defy the will and purpose of God, who is working to save the world. It is for this reason, although God is never mentioned in the story of Esther, that the wicked Haman cannot carry out his plan to destroy the Jews. Throughout Esther's story there is the underlying assumption that God's chosen people cannot be eliminated. Even if Esther had not come to their rescue, "deliverance will rise for the Jews from another quarter," as Mordecai tells her (4:14). And we read in 9:2 that "no one could stand against them" throughout the whole Persian Empire. The reason is that they are God's people, servants of his sovereign purpose in the world.

I have the sneaking suspicion that is the reason why the Jews have never been eliminated in history. They have been hounded to the ends of the earth, persecuted by all manner of persons and governments, faced with seemingly overwhelming odds against their survival. But the Jews are God's people, as are all faithful Christians in the covenant, and as Second Isaiah proclaimed to his compatriots in exile, they cannot be consumed because God is with them (Isa 43:1–3). If the Jews are ever destroyed from the face of the earth, then God's purpose for his creation has been defeated, and indeed, there is no sovereign God who is Lord over all. But God is Lord, and his purpose will be fulfilled, and finally all will acknowledge his good rule.

Esther therefore is a little story told to acknowledge all these facts. It is a triumphant tale, in which the enemies of the Jews are slaughtered. And we have been taught as Christians that we are to love our enemies and to pray for those who persecute us (Matt 5:44). Esther is celebrated at Purim by our Jewish brothers and sisters, because it is a reminder of the persistence of Jewish life, despite persecution, in the purpose of God. It is a testimony to God's lordship over all peoples and nations.

91

PART TWO

Writings

❧ 16 ❧

"Skin for Skin"

JOB 2:1–10

*T*HIS IS THE STATED OLD TESTAMENT READING FOR THE
twenty-seventh Sunday of Pentecost or Ordinary Time
in Cycle B of the three-year common lectionary. It affords a
wonderful entrance into the theological depths of the Book
of Job, but people often question its characterization of God.
The Lord turns over the care of Job to "Satan" and deliberately allows that figure to bring unutterable suffering upon
an innocent man. How are we to understand that?

Plumbing the Text

Job 2:1–10 is inextricably connected with Job 1, and we
cannot understand the text without discussing that initial
chapter also. We read in Job 1:1 that Job is from "the land of
Uz." That country has never been identified, and the story
of Job is intentionally separated from all specific mentions of
historical times and places. In short, it is intended for all
persons everywhere.

Similarly, in 1:6 and 2:1 we find the phrase, "there was
a day." That has the same meaning as the familiar "Once upon
a time," and it is clear that the story is meant to be just
that—a story, a popular tale, rather than an historical account.
We are reading a make-believe story, with a following extended cycle of dialogues, that is meant to pose a problem to

our minds and hearts. The question to ask of Job, therefore, is not, "Would God do such a thing?" but rather, "What is the author of this story telling us about our relation to God?"

We find from ch. 1 that Job is a very rich man (1:2–3) and from ch. 29 that he was highly respected by all. Above all, Job is "blameless and upright" (1:1). The parallel to that statement in the verse tells us what that means. Job is blameless in that he "fears God," that is, he worships God in spirit and in truth. And he is upright because he turns away from all evil and exercises right conduct along a straight path. He is a pious man whose morality springs out of and matches his piety. Indeed, so pious and upright is he that he even offers burnt offerings on behalf of his children on the days after their birthdays, to cover any sins that they might have committed (1:5).

The central problem of the book is set forth by the dialogue between the Lord and "Satan" in 1:12. We must be very clear, however, that the translation "Satan" does not point to the devil or a demonic figure. There is a definite article before the word in the Hebrew, indicating that it is not a name but a title, and it is more correctly translated as "The Adversary." Moreover, he is a member of God's heavenly court and counted as one of God's messengers, so he is not a leader of the forces of evil, as the figure of Satan later became. Rather, The Adversary's basic duty is to go about the earth and to accuse human beings before God. We might say that he is a superhuman "Attorney General," sent by God to call sinners to account.

The setting of the dialogue in both chs. 1 and 2 is the heavenly assembly that is a familiar concept in the Old Testament. God is pictured as enthroned in the heaven of heavens, as the King of the universe. He is surrounded by the heavenly beings, or "sons of God," who act as his messengers for various duties on earth. (For other pictures of the heavenly assembly, see 1 Kgs 22:19–23; Isa 6:1–8, etc.)

In the dialogue, God points out to The Adversary how blameless and upright is his servant Job, assuming that The Adversary can bring no accusation against that righteous man.

But The Adversary poses the central question of the book. "Does Job fear God for nought?" (Job 1:9). That is, is Job blameless and upright because God rewards him for his piety and morality with all the blessings of a good life? Certainly that is the theology of some Wisdom Literature, of which the Book of Job is a part. The righteous are rewarded, the evil are punished by God. And that is the theology of the friends of Job who dialogue with him from ch. 4 on.

God, however, has faith in his servant Job, and to prove that The Adversary is mistaken about Job, God allows The Adversary to destroy in a day all of Job's belongings and children (1:13–19). Job responds to these calamities in traditional rites of mourning (1:20) that ease his grief and that allow him to bow to God's will and to bless God (1:21). God is good, in Job's eyes, and he will charge him with no wrong (1:22).

Our text in 2:1–10, then, repeats the setting and dialogue of ch. 1, but the problem is deepened. The Adversary maintains that Job will curse God if Job can save his own life by doing so. "Skin for skin," says The Adversary. That is, when everything that Job is and has ("skin") is taken away from him, he will curse God if it will enable him to save his own skin (2:4).

The Lord, still believing in his servant Job, therefore allows The Adversary to inflict Job from head to foot with loathsome sores. Job's self is attacked bodily and changed into repugnance. He loses his self, his appearance, his self-identity, his consciousness of who he is. He is devastated in body and soul, so that all he can do is sit in the city dump, to which lepers were banished, and scrape at his itching sores with broken pieces of pottery.

Job's wife, who is supposed to be his mutual helper (Gen 2:18), instead becomes the helper of The Adversary, advising Job to curse God and die (2:9). It does not pay to trust and obey God (cf. Mal 3:17; it seems probable that the Book of Job comes out of the same post-exilic era, ca. 450 B.C.). Obviously God has cast Job off. Job should do the same and be rid of his Lord by dying. But Job clings to his relationship with God and maintains that God, in his wisdom, may send evil as well as good (2:10; cf. Isa 45:7; 41:23; Zeph 1:12; Jer 18:7–10).

Forming the Sermon

Why do we worship and obey God? That is the central problem of the Book of Job. Do we go to church and pray and try to follow the Lord's commandments because we believe that the Lord will therefore reward us for our piety? That was standard Wisdom Theology, against which the Book of Job is a profound protest, but a lot of good people in the church hold that attitude. Televanglists continually admonish us from the TV screen to believe in Jesus so that we may have success in our business or health in our bodies or peace in our families.

Some years ago the *Presbyterian Outlook* reported that a man in Dade County, Florida was suing his church for the return of the eight hundred dollars that he had contributed to it. "On September 7," he said in his court suit, "I delivered $800 to the . . . Church in response to the pastor's promise that blessings, benefits and rewards would come to the person who did tithe ten per cent of his wealth. I did not and have not received those benefits." Such is the selfish piety that believes God will reward good deeds. Job however teaches differently.

Certainly there is a deeper level of devotion to the Lord that worships and obeys God in grateful response to all of the blessings that God has bestowed. Gratitude to God for life and loved ones, for meaningful work and peaceful rest, for food and shelter and the beauty of nature and the comfort of community overflows in trustful obedience for all of God's benefits.

> Bless the LORD, O my soul,
>   and forget not all his benefits,
> who forgives all your iniquity,
>   who heals all your diseases,
> who redeems your life from the Pit,
>   who crowns you with steadfast love and mercy,

who satisfies you with good as long as you live
  so that your youth is renewed like the eagle's.
                                    (Psalm 103:2–5)

Every true worshiper of the Lord can say "Amen" to that
psalm. We love and obey God because he has first loved us
(1 John 4:19). That is a source of genuine piety.

But all of the benefits of God bestowed upon ordinary
persons apparently have been taken away from Job, and he is
left bereft of family, friends, and goods, clinging only miser-
ably to life on an ash heap. Is there still a deeper reason to
trust and worship God?

Job apparently thinks so, for he will not relinquish his
relationship with his Maker. Indeed, he cries out for the
maintenance of that relationship.

Oh, that I knew where I might find him,
  that I might come even to his seat! (Job 23:3;
        cf. 9:11, 34; 13:3, 20–24; 30:20; 31:35)

Job has known a communion and fellowship with God that
most persons never know, days when God watched over him,
when by God's light he walked through darkness, and when
the friendship of God was upon his tent (Job 29:1–4). Then
Job was with God continually, knowing him intimately.

I think such friendship with God comes only from im-
mersing oneself in God's Word, communing with him continually in silent prayer, and seeing one's every action as a
service to God. We saw such a friendship and love for God in
Mother Teresa, but it is a friendship that can be had by every
person.

In such a relationship, there is no thought of reward.
God is loved and trusted and obeyed simply because God is
lovable and trustworthy and good. God is loved for himself
beyond all benefit that one might gain. Surely there is something of that in the phrase of the Shorter Catechism when it
says that the chief goal of all of our living is to glorify God *and
enjoy him forever.* The deepest piety *enjoys* God!

When disaster strikes, therefore, as it struck Job, the
truest worshipers can still say, "God is good." When pain

99

overwhelms, they can yet know that "underneath are the everlasting arms" (Deut 33:27). When death approaches, they yet affirm that their Redeemer lives and that they shall meet him face to face (Job 19:25–27; cf. 1 Cor 13:12). And the friendship with God that has been known and trusted endures beyond the grave.

> Whom have I in heaven but thee?
>> And there is nothing upon earth that I desire besides thee.
> My flesh and my heart may fail,
>> but God is the strength of my heart and my portion forever. (Ps 73:25–26)

The sufferer Job knew a fellowship with God that outlasted all his misery. Over-against his supposedly wise friends and The Adversary, who believed that piety should expect a reward, Job clung to his fellowship with his Maker in the face of doubt and degradation and death. And in the end, Job's faith was vindicated and his friends and The Adversary proved wrong (Job 42:1–9).

The deepest love of God comes from the intimate knowledge that God is simply lovable—in his care for his creatures, in his magnificent might, shown in all creation, in his stooping to speak with a devastated man who sits in a city dump (Job 38–41). We worship a God who is Love—Love finally manifested in the Son of God who took all our suffering upon himself. And in that Love, freely given apart from all our deserving, persons like Job and we have life and have it eternally.

❧ 17 ❧

"When Israel Went Forth from Egypt"

PSALM 114

*I*N THE THREE-YEAR LECTIONARY, THERE IS A LISTING OF several texts that might be used for the first celebration of Easter at the Vigil before the dawn of Easter day. This psalm is last in the list and is paired with the resurrection accounts in all three Synoptic Gospels. As such, that is an inspired choice, for no Old Testament reading could better set forth the awe and joy associated with the resurrection of Christ, and few Old Testament readings could better join Old Testament and New as the account of the one saving history.

Plumbing the Text

In later Judaism, this psalm was read on the eighth day of the Passover festival, and the reason for that seems clear. Psalm 114 concentrates on the exodus of Israel out of slavery in Egypt and the events that followed that exodus.

Verse 1 emphasizes the former bondage of Israel, not by recounting their sufferings under slavery, but by pointing to the fact that they were slaves to "barbarians," people who spoke a foreign tongue that the Israelites could not understand. The people who were supremely people of the Word were enslaved by those who spoke unintelligible words.

Verse 2 centers in on the election of Israel as God's chosen people. There is no separation between Israel and Judah. They are one people, descended from Jacob, and chosen to be the people with whom God dwells. This is a reference not to the dwelling of God in the temple on Zion but to the fact that God goes with them continually. "I will be with you," he had promised Moses (Exod 3:12). "I will be your God and you will be my people," he had promised in the covenant. And so he went before them in a pillar of cloud by day and a pillar of fire by night as they trekked through the terrors of the wilderness (Exod 13:21–22). Indeed, it was in God's going with them that Israel was distinct from all other peoples on earth (Exod 33:16). God chose Israel to be the recipients of his continual presence, to be his "own possession," his "peculiar treasure" (Exod 19:6 KJV) among all the nations of the earth. That is the emphasis of v. 2 of our text.

When God set his love upon his people (cf. Deut 7:7) and manifested his power over the empire of Egypt by delivering Israel, not only his lordship over empires was revealed, however, but also his lordship over all of nature (vv. 3–4). The Reed Sea saw him and fled before him, its waters rolled back to allow Israel to pass through on dry land (Exod 14:22). The Jordan knew its Lord and ceased in its flow (Josh 3:14–17; 4:23–24). Mount Sinai quaked when God descended upon it (Exod 19:18), and the hills skipped like rams in a pasture before his presence (cf. Ps 29:6).

Indeed, God in his relation with Israel showed himself Lord of all—God of gods (cf. Exod 12:12), Lord over nature, Ruler of all peoples. And so v. 7 of our psalm calls on the entire earth to tremble before the might and glory of the omnipotent One of Jacob (cf. Ps 96:9; 99:1, etc.). The Lord is awesome in his power and majesty.

Yet, it is precisely this awesome, mighty Ruler of all who condescends to be with his people and who bends to give them aid in their extremities (v. 8). When they wander through the dry and desolate desert and have no water to drink, the Lord provides them water from a rock that they may live (Exod 17:6; cf. Num 20:11). The mighty Lord of all is also the Savior of his people.

Forming the Sermon

Is there a better description of our God who raises Jesus Christ from the dead? Certainly he is showing himself Lord over empires when the women discover that empty tomb on Easter morn. Jesus died at the hands of the Roman Empire's executioners. He had been sentenced to death by the Roman prefect, Pontius Pilate, the fifth governor of the province of Judea, who was concerned for his own position and reputation. But God raised his Son and showed that his will triumphed over even Rome's.

When God emptied the tomb, he revealed himself to be Lord over nature also. It is not natural for human beings to rise from the dead. The laws of the natural world consign all things and persons to die; everything hastens to its end. But the God who created nature's order and who set its laws in motion is not bound by our observations of what is natural, nor is he determined by the limits of what he himself has created. He is Sovereign over nature's ways, and he is the Lord of life and death, bringing forth a resurrection when such seemed impossible. It is no wonder that the women at the tomb were afraid and awe struck when they heard, "He is not here; for he has risen" (Matt 28:6).

In fact, there is a note in the accounts of the resurrection that link it closely with our psalm. As the women approach the tomb of Jesus on Easter morning, they wonder how they will roll away the stone that seals the tomb so that they may anoint Jesus' dead body. In Mark and Luke, the women find the stone already rolled aside and the angel(s) tell them that Christ has risen. But in Matthew's account we read, "And behold, there was a great earthquake; for an angel of the Lord descended from heaven and came and rolled back the stone . . ." (Matt 28:2). "The mountains skipped like rams, the hills like lambs." God shook the earth at the resurrection of his Son as he shook it also at the sea and at Sinai.

103

It is appropriate, therefore, to sound the imperative of Ps 114 on Easter Eve. "Tremble, O earth, at the presence of the LORD, at the presence of the God of Jacob." Or as Ps 99 puts it, "The LORD reigns; let the people tremble" (v. 1)! God reigns over all history and nature at the resurrection of our Lord. Human powers and human beings could not defeat him. All of our sins gathered together to pound the nails through his hands on that cross, and we in our pride thought that we had done with God forever. But God's Son forgave us our sin and was raised triumphant over it, forever the victor over earth's death and all its evil. And now nothing in heaven or on earth can deter him until he is acknowledged as Lord of all by every bowed knee and confessing tongue.

The miracle, though, the awesome miracle beyond Christ's resurrection from the dead, is that this God, this Lord of all, has chosen us along with Israel to be his own possession and to be with us all our lives. Seeing our thirst in the wilderness of our days, our longing for guidance and meaning and good, he has stooped to give us drink from the living water of his Spirit (cf. John 4:10–15). And that water gives us a "spring of water welling up to eternal life" (John 4:14). Because Christ lives, we too can live—abundantly, joyfully, eternally—if we live in him through trust in his working in us.

live in Christ = trust in his working in us

❧ 18 ❧

"By the Waters of Babylon"

PSALM 137

MANY PEOPLE LOVE THE BEAUTIFUL BEGINNING OF THIS
psalm, "By the waters of Babylon," and countless sermons have lifted out the words of v. 4 to speak of singing the
Lord's song in a strange land. Some congregations are accustomed to reading vv. 1–6 as a responsive reading. But I know
of no liturgy that has included vv. 7–9, with the last hate-
filled v. 9, "Happy shall he be who takes your little ones/ and
dashes them against the rock!" There is the general feeling
that such thoughts should not occur in the Bible. Nevertheless, there is valuable preaching material to be used from this
psalm, and it is listed in the three-year lectionary as an
alternate reading for the twenty-seventh Sunday in Pentecost
or Ordinary Time in Cycle C.

Plumbing the Text

Psalm 137 is divided into three stanzas, vv. 1–3, 4–6, and
7–9. Verses 1–3 deal with the past, vv. 4–6 with the present,
and vv. 7–9 with the future. In other words, the Psalmist is
still in Babylonia. Jerusalem still lies in ruins, before the Jews
return from Babylonian exile in about 535 B.C. and begin the
task of rebuilding. The author looks back, in vv. 1–3, to the
hardships Israel has already suffered during the exile.

To be sure, many Israelites adjusted well to their captivity in Babylonia and did not undergo extreme hardships. They had their own communities, and they developed a good number of commercial, agricultural, and cultural enterprises. Some of them even became wealthy, and many of them refused to return to Palestine after the liberating decree of Cyrus of Persia in 538 B.C. While in Babylonia the Israelites developed many of the religious and legal institutions of Judaism, including the massive Babylonian Talmud, which is a commentary on the Hebrew code of laws (the Mishnah) and which became authoritative for most of Judaism.

The singers of this psalm, however, bitterly remember the taunts of Israel's Babylonian captors, who forced them to sing Songs of Zion as an entertainment for their captors' amusement. Some have suggested that the songs demanded were simply the general hymns of praise of God that are so numerous in the Psalter. But as we shall see, I am more inclined to think that the captors demanded those specific songs that related to Jerusalem with its temple as God's dwelling-place. Some of those Songs of Zion are now found in our Psalter (Ps 46, 48, 76, 84, 87, 122).

From the plural pronouns of the first stanza of our passage, the second stanza switches to the singular, with the Psalmist remembering the ruin of Jerusalem. He vows never to forget the Jerusalem that was—and that still is for him—God's city and therefore his highest joy. If he does forget, he asks God to wither his right hand that plays the lyre or harp, and to paralyze his tongue that sings the Songs of Zion.

Looking toward the future, the Psalmist then asks God to remember that it was the Edomites who joined in the destruction and pillaging of Jerusalem at the time of the Babylonian conquest of the city. From the very first, Edom was an enemy of Israel. This enmity was foreshadowed in the hatred of Esau, Edom's forebear, for Jacob, Israel's forebear (Gen 25:29–34; 27; 32–36). Though the Edomites were brothers to the Israelites, and though the law forbade hatred of Edom (Deut 23:7), the enmity between the two continued throughout Israel's history and was magnified when the

Edomites gloated over Jerusalem's downfall, looted the city, and betrayed escaping Israelites to the Babylonians (Obad 12–14). The Psalmist is asking, in v. 7, that the Lord remember that perfidy and punish Edom accordingly.

Babylonia, however, was the principal devastator of Jerusalem, breaking down its walls, burning its dwellings and temple, looting its treasures, and carrying all but its poorest peasants into exile. And Babylonia is still the ruling empire at the time of this psalm. Therefore, remembering what Nebuchadrezzar II and his troops did to Jerusalem, plural voices join in the song in vv. 8 and 9, perhaps in response to the singular voice of v. 7. They curse Babylon and wish for it the gory destruction of its children so that it will no longer exist.[1]

Forming the Sermon

If we ask what principally is expressed in Ps 137, it is not bitterness over suffering at the hands of the Babylonians, nor is it anguish over the destruction of Judah's capitol city. Rather, it is religious zeal for the honor of God.

Jerusalem was not important to Israel because it was a beautiful city or the center of Israel's Davidic monarchy or the hub of Israel's commercial and cultural life. Jerusalem was important because on its hill of Zion stood the temple of Solomon. And in that temple, in its Holy of Holies, rested the Ark of the Covenant that formed the base of the throne of God. God dwelt in the midst of his people, invisibly enthroned above the cherubim's wings that overspread the ark from each end (1 Sam 4:4; 1 Kgs 8:1–21).

Moreover, because God dwelt in the temple in the midst of his people, the Songs of Zion celebrated God's defense of Jerusalem. "God is in the midst of her," reads Ps 46:5, "she shall not be moved." "Within [Jerusalem's] citadel, God has shown himself a sure defense" (Ps 48:3). Jerusalem is "the city of our God, which God establishes forever" (Ps 48:8). "The LORD is a sun and shield" (Ps 84:11). "He cuts off the spirit of princes" and "is terrible to the kings of the earth"

(Ps 76:12). God, the Lord dwelling in Jerusalem, was the guarantee of Israel's life.

But in this psalm, Jerusalem is nothing but rubble, the psalms of Zion were sung merely as entertainment for foreigners, the Ark of the Covenant has been lost, and God's defense of Israel has amounted to nothing. In short, God has been dishonored as one who has not saved his people. "Where is your God?" the Babylonians jeer (Ps 79:10; cf. Lam 2:15). "Why hasn't he defended Jerusalem?" "Doesn't he have the power?" "Your psalm said Jerusalem would never be moved." "We moved it, didn't we? Ha, ha, ha!" Those are the taunts and scorn that eat at the Psalmist's soul. God is on trial in this psalm, and he seems to have been defeated. That cannot help but remind us of the jeering that took place at the foot of Jesus' cross.

> And those who passed by derided him, wagging their heads, and saying, "Aha! You who would destroy the temple and build it in three days, save yourself, and come down from the cross!" So also the chief priests mocked him to one another with the scribes, saying, "He saved others; he cannot save himself. Let the Christ, the King of Israel, come down now from the cross, that we may see and believe." (Mark 15:29–32)

For the disciples of Jesus, God was on trial there too, as he was for the exiles in Babylonia.

Contrary to the disciples, who were sure that Jesus' death was the end of their hopes for God's redemption of Israel (cf. Luke 24:31), our Psalmist retains the belief that despite the sufferings of the exile and despite Jerusalem's ruined condition, God is still the Lord in charge of events. Verses 5–7 are really an affirmation of the Psalmist's continuing faith in the Lord. God is still present in the midst of his people, and so Jerusalem is still the Psalmist's highest joy. And God can still act as Lord over the nations, remembering the treachery of the Edomites at the time of the fall of Jerusalem and judging them for their deeds. Our Psalmist has not lost his faith or his hope for the future. That is the same faith and hope that all faithful people of God have retained in the midst of suffering and ruin. God is the Ruler yet, though all the evidence seems against it.

108

We should note that the call for vengeance upon Edom is directed to God in v. 7. The Psalmist is not taking matters into his own hands. Rather, he is turning over all retribution to the Lord. We find such prayers very frequently in the Psalter. "Make them bear their guilt, O God," prays the speaker in Ps 5:10, "let them fall by their own counsels." "Let them be caught in the schemes which they have devised," prays another (Ps 10:2). Or, "May their belly be filled with what thou has stored up for them" (Ps 17:14). Or "Requite them according to their work,/ and according to the evil of their deeds;/ requite them according to the work of their hands;/ render them their due reward" (Ps 28:4). We find the same prayer on the lips of the prophet Jeremiah when his neighbors and friends try to kill him: "O LORD of hosts, who judgest righteously,/ who triest the heart and the mind,/ let me see thy vengeance upon them,/ for to thee I have committed my cause" (Jer 11:20).

Paul wrote the church at Rome, "Beloved, never avenge yourselves, but leave it to the wrath of God; for it is written, 'Vengeance is mine, I will repay, says the Lord' " (Rom 12:19; cf. Heb 10:30). These Psalmists and Jeremiah and Paul too leave any and all retribution up to God, to do what he will. They therefore prevent building up in themselves that hatred and spirit of revenge that eats at the hearts and souls of so many people and that finally ruins those people's own lives. Indeed, Paul counsels that by leaving all to God, we may heap burning coals upon an enemy's head—that is, coals of repentance that lead to peace.

Given the fact that the Psalmist, in v. 7 of our passage, turns retribution over to the Lord, it is difficult to believe that the words of vv. 8–9 come from his lips. Rather, I believe they are responses of others to the Psalmist's words in vv. 4–7, and they speak an entirely different message. These speakers themselves want revenge for what the Babylonians did to them in the destruction of Jerusalem and the exile, and they utter bloodthirsty curses on that nation. There is no trust in God's requital in such expressions. Hatred toward Babylonia is spit out from hating hearts. It is also doubtful that such

109

hatred stems from a concern for God's honor and glory. The Psalmist of vv. 4–7 was concerned above all that God, the Lord in Zion, be honored as Ruler over all. These speakers in vv. 8–9 are concerned only for themselves and their own hurt.

Maybe that tells us something about hatred—that it never honors God or is concerned with his lordship. It is centered solely in human hearts that are concerned only for themselves. And perhaps that is the reason that our Lord, dying on his cross while the mob below his feet jeers and scorns him, responds not in hatred for his executioners and mockers but with words of forgiveness, "Father, forgive them, for they know not what they do" (Luke 23:34). That prayer acknowledges that God is still in charge of everything that is happening, and it glorifies and honors God for the loving and forgiving Lord that he is. It is good to be concerned for the reputation of God, as our Psalmists of vv. 1–7 were deeply concerned. And we enlarge God's reputation throughout the world by telling all nations what God has done. But our zeal for God's glory cannot cause us to sink into hatred, not even for our enemies or for those whom we think are God's enemies. Leave the enemies to God. Trust that he is in fact the Lord. For by so doing we will glorify God's holy name.

Notes

1. We are told that such treatment of children was the practice of Hazael of Syria (2 Kgs 8:12), of the Medes (Isa 13:16, 18), and of the Assyrians (Nah 3:10). Cf. Hos 13:16. During the Second World War, Nazi troops also were reported to have killed infants in such a manner.

❦ 19 ❦

Sophia

PROVERBS 8:1–4, 22–31

THIS IS THE STATED OLD TESTAMENT LESSON FOR TRINITY
Sunday in Cycle C of the three-year common lectionary.
As such, it is paired with Rom 5:1–5 and John 16:12–15, both
of which mention the three persons of the Trinity: Father,
Son, and Holy Spirit. Because Jesus Christ is the wisdom of
God (1 Cor 1:30), it is possible to use this text for Trinity
Sunday. But the passage also affords the opportunity to deal
with the Sophia cult that has sprung up among radical femi-
nists in our time.

Plumbing the Text

The Hebrew word for wisdom is *hokmah*, the Greek
translation is *sophia*. Wisdom teachings were known throughout the ancient Near East, and they appear in the Old Testament primarily in the Book of Proverbs, although they can be
found in many passages in both Old and New Testaments.

In standard Wisdom Theology it is believed that God
sets certain orders and structures into creation and that these
are the ways in which all the natural world and the world of
human relationships work. The wise person is one who observes these ways or learns them from sages and accommo-
dates his or her life to them. But the person who will not learn
such wisdom is a fool and will not find the good life. All

persons are invited to seek and to learn wisdom, which can be gained from experience and keen observation.

In Prov 1–9 wisdom is personified as a female figure, replacing the figure of the teacher and sage to speak on her own behalf. She is variously described as the one calling or preaching in the streets (1:20; 8:1); as a guide, guardian, and conversationalist (6:22); as a sister or intimate friend (7:4); as a hostess inviting others to her table (9:1–6). She calls to human beings, inviting them to listen to her, to heed her summons, to seek her out (our stated text, as well as 8:4–5, 10, 32–36). She woos human beings, promising them knowledge and love (8:9, 17), riches and honor (8:18, 21), righteousness and justice (8:20), equity (2:9), security (1:33), and life (8:35).

More important, in our text, wisdom is described as the first work of creation (8:22–23), who was present with God when he made all else, who was his darling child, rejoicing and dancing before him and delighting in his works, including his creation of human beings (vv. 30–31).

We must note very carefully, however, that in our text in Proverbs and in the rest of the Old Testament, personified wisdom is not divine or a hypostasis or an incarnation of God: The monotheistic Hebrew Scriptures would never accept such a doctrine. Wisdom is personified only as a creature. She has been created before all other things and is therefore different from God's other creatures. She reveals the ways of God—of love and righteousness and life—that are built into the structure of the universe. Indeed, we would not go wrong if we characterized wisdom as the plan of God, whereby he has ordered all the natural world and directed the course of human history. Thus in the apocryphal first-century-B.C. book the Wisdom of Solomon, it is said that by wisdom (i.e., by God's plan) God has done his acts of salvation on behalf of Israel. Wisdom "pervades and permeates all things" (Wis 7:24), she makes all things new (Wis 7:27), and evil cannot triumph over her (Wis 7:30). Such is the figure that is here presented in our text and that is then enlarged in apocryphal works.

Forming the Sermon

For several decades we have had in this country what is known as the "women's movement." It reaches back as far as the nineteenth century, but after women gained the right to vote in 1920, it died out until the civil rights movement of the 1960s. At that time women, spurred on by such publications as Betty Friedan's *The Feminine Mystique,* began rightly to organize and press for equal status, compensation, and rights in both society and church. A lot has happened since that initial push for equality, much of which has had a profound effect on the life of the Christian church.

Radical feminist women in the church, and especially in the Roman Catholic Church, began to question traditional Christian theology. They challenged the supposedly male God of the Scriptures, who was incarnated in a male savior and who rules over a hierarchy of males-females-children-animals-nature. It was that hierarchy, the feminists claimed, that had led to the subjection of women. While acknowledging that the God of the Bible has no sexuality, the radical feminists set out to re-imagine a God more to their liking.

God, they said, is not a transcendent ruler over the world of nature and history. God is immanent, contained in our world, and identical with the vital sources of life that we find in the natural world and in each other. God is better thought of as a female, a mother, a friend, a lover. She is the great Primal Matrix, the ground of being, from which all things have been birthed and to which all will return at death.[1] She permeates all things and persons, and she connects all of them together, so that we are all bundled together in one great matrix of life. The goddess can be known through the experience of anyone who seeks her, and she is to be worshiped as the source of all being. Thus, a special revelation of the goddess is not necessary; the Bible need not be used.

What is the name of this re-imagined goddess? Some call her Mother, but lately radical feminists have decided that she is Sophia, and they have pointed to both our text in Proverbs and to apocryphal works as the basis of that naming.

113

Certainly wisdom, sophia, is a natural figure for the radical feminists to have an affinity for. She is feminine, she pervades all things and persons, she can be known through experience, and she gives life and knowledge and love. She is "the connectedness between all things,"[2] and so she can be that goddess, that matrix of being, that universal consciousness that the radical feminists have re-imagined as God. Sophia or wisdom, who is only a creature in Proverbs, has been turned into a female deity. She is in, through, and under all things, she is available to feminists' reflection on their own experience, she promises them life and well-being, and it is she whom they worship in their liturgies.

What we must realize, however, is that as the radical feminists have portrayed Sophia, they have made her into a mythological figure that has no basis in fact. As Elisabeth Johnson has written, "Portrayed as sister, mother, bride, hostess, female beloved, woman prophet, teacher, and friend, but above all as divine spirit, Sophia's portrait has its roots in the Great Goddess of the ancient Near Eastern world."[3] In short, the concept of a divine Sophia comes from a myth. She is a figment of imagination.

Jews and Christians do not worship a myth, however, and so when they considered the figure of wisdom in Proverbs, they connected wisdom with historical events. True wisdom, said Judaism in the later Book of Ecclesiasticus, is the Torah, God's specific revelation of himself to his covenant people, given within the sphere of history (24:23, 32, 33). But the New Testament goes further than that. It says that Jesus Christ, the Word of God incarnate, is wisdom. "God is the source of your life in Christ Jesus," wrote Paul, "whom God made our wisdom, our righteousness and sanctification and redemption" (1 Cor 1:30). Thus, Jesus frequently uses wisdom sayings in the New Testament. And in the Gospel according to John, those acts that are ascribed to the figure of wisdom in the Old Testament are ascribed to Jesus Christ. He is the source of true knowledge, of true life, of the true way to the Father.

Our Christian faith is rooted firmly in the sphere of actual history. We did not make it up. Jesus of Nazareth was not some mythological, feminine, amorphous matrix of being, incarnated in all things and persons. No, Jesus was an historical figure of flesh and blood, a descendant of Abraham and David, who walked the dusty roads of Palestine, who gave his life for the sins of the world, and who was raised from the dead to conquer the grave forever for those who trust in him. He alone is God with us, Immanuel, and the worship of some goddess called Sophia is an idolatrous breaking of the first of the Ten Commandments.

Notes

1. Rosemary Radford Ruether, *Sexism and God-Talk: Toward a Feminist Theology* (Boston: Beacon, 1983).
2. Susan Cady, Marian Roman, Hal Taussig, *Sophia* (San Francisco: Harper & Row, 1989), 5.
3. *She Who Is: The Mystery of God in Feminist Theological Discourse* (New York: Crossroad, 1992), 98.

❧ 20 ❧

"Arise, My Love"

SONG OF SONGS 2:8–13

IT IS REMARKABLE THAT THIS PASSAGE IS A STATED OLD Testament lesson in the three-year common lectionary. Preachers usually ignore Song of Songs. Nevertheless, this text is the Old Testament lesson for the twenty-second Sunday of Pentecost or Ordinary Time in Cycle B. Rarely are sermons heard on the passage, and yet it forms a wonderful opportunity for dealing with romantic love, a subject that engrosses our society.

Plumbing the Text

The Song of Songs (which means "the best song") is what we might call an anthology of romantic and often very sensual love poetry. The book has no apparent order to it, nor does it come from the hand of one author. Its date and place of origin remain uncertain, and all scholars agree that it was not written by King Solomon. Rather it has the characteristic of simple, naive folk poetry, in the form of romantic monologues and dialogues. The speakers in the poems are not named, and the setting of the various poems changes frequently and abruptly.

The collection was incorporated into the canon very late as a part of the Writings, whose final form was not accepted until after A.D. 70. Song of Songs does not mention God and is therefore not a religious work. But it was put into the canon because it was given an allegorical interpretation. The lovers in the poems came to be understood as God and Israel, while in the Christian church, the book was interpreted as expressions of the love between Christ and his church or between Christ and the individual Christian. To be true to the actual meaning of the book, however, it should be viewed simply as what it is—love poetry.

In Song of Songs 2:8–13, it is springtime, and a young man in the bloom and strength of youth comes running across the hills to his beloved's house and stands outside her window, calling her to come away with him to a lover's tryst. The winter rains are over, nature is in glorious flower, and young love is eager.

One line of this text is well-known: "the voice of the turtledove is heard in our land" (2:12c). The King James Version incorrectly reads, "the voice of the turtle," and Hollywood even produced a movie called "Summertime," starring Katherine Hepburn, which played on that theme. Many used to wonder what sound a turtle made, but it was romantic to think that even a turtle sought a lover.

Forming the Sermon

Sermons on this text often use an allegorical interpretation of it. Most recently, I heard a sermon that used analogy: As a young lover yearns to be with his beloved, so we should yearn to be with God. True love is attentive and faithful and responsive, and so should our love be to God.

Most profitably, however, the text should be interpreted for what it is—a young man in spring, calling out his fair beloved to accompany him to the hills. Anyone who has ever been in love knows the eagerness and longing of that scene and can identify immediately with the text. But what does that say to us about the Bible and faith?

First, because this book of love poetry is in our canon, it is clear that the Bible puts its stamp of approval on sexual desire and love. For centuries, the church tried to avoid that

117

fact, even elevating chastity or celibacy to the rank of a higher form of devotion to God. Sex, with its impulses and desires, became something "dirty," a sordid surrender to the flesh, apart from any spiritual good.

Already in the Book of Genesis, however, the desire of the sexes for one another is understood as a good gift of a loving God. After the creation of Adam, in Gen 2, the Lord muses that it is "not good for the man to be alone" (v. 18). Adam needs a corresponding partner, one in whom he sees himself, one with whom he can share and care and commune (which is the meaning of a "helper fit for him" in Gen 2:18). The Lord therefore causes a deep sleep to come upon the man, and out of the man's rib, he makes a woman. The two were once one, you see, and after the woman's creation, they long to become one again. So when the Lord brings the woman to the man, Adam cries out in an ecstatic cry, "This, this at last, is bone of my bones and flesh of my flesh. Here at last is one corresponding to me with whom I can share my life and love." The two become "one flesh" in the joyful new community of marital love. And, adds the Scripture, they "were both naked and they were not ashamed" (vv. 23–25).

The body, the desire of the sexes for one another, the resulting one flesh in the sexual consummation of marriage—these are good gifts of a loving God who desires that we have life and have it abundantly. And the abundance of that life of marital love is then celebrated, for example, in Song of Songs 4:9–5:1. As that passage shows, marital love can involve tenderness and admiration of the beloved, sensual pleasure, and the highest forms of human joy. God has given us sexual love as a good gift that can unite husband and wife as one in a pleasurable, refreshing, exhilarating oneness.

Like all of God's good gifts, however, sexual desire and love are to be received and used only according to God's ordinances for them. In our text, the vigorous young man yearns to be with his fair beloved, as all young lovers yearn to be with one another. And as we all know, sexual desire is part of that yearning. But there is no doubt whatsoever that, in the Scriptures, sexual intercourse is to be employed only within the bonds of marriage. Adultery is specifically forbidden in the Ten Commandments, which are the most basic commands for the people of God (Exod 20:14; Deut 5:18). And fornication, that is, pre-marital sexual intercourse, is condemned by Jesus (Mark 7:21 and parallels) and Paul (Gal 5:19). Paul states that fornication excludes one from the Kingdom of God (1 Cor 6:9). Indeed, all forms of sexual aberrations are forbidden, including seduction, rape, sodomy, bestiality, incest, homosexuality, and prostitution (Lev 19:20–22, 29; 20:10–21; Deut 22:22), such acts often being grouped together in the New Testament under the general term "immorality" (1 Cor 6:9; 2 Cor 12:21; Eph 5:5; Col 3:5; 1 Thess 4:3–8; 1 Tim 1:10; Heb 13:4). God has intended sexual intercourse as a unifying act within the covenant of marriage only.

That such limitations on the use of our sexuality are manifestations of God's love for us cannot be doubted. For example, God commands "You shall not commit adultery" because he knows that an adulterous relationship will undermine the trust necessary for a marriage and will make a happy marital life impossible. Similarly, God forbids pre-marital sexual intercourse, because he knows that at the basis of all lasting marital relations is the total commitment of self, of which sexual union is the outward sign. Marriage is like no other human covenant in its total, lifelong commitment. God guards marriage by his commandments for it. And he does so because he wants us to know the joy of a lifelong, faithful marital union, in which husband and wife grow together in love and companionship and knowledge of each other through the years. God wants it to go well with us (cf. Deut 5:29). God wants for us only good. And so he gives us his commandments as the guide to the happiness he desires for us.

Human love of male and female, celebrated in our text, is a wondrous gift that enriches our lives if it is exercised according to God's commands. Otherwise it can end in disaster and heartbreak for all concerned. Indeed, God calls the failure of marital love due to adultery "violence" (Mal 2:16), because it does violence to the hopes and dreams and deepest emotions of those involved.

119

We might note one other characteristic of the Song of
Songs. While it is the male who speaks in our particular text,
throughout this book, there is mutuality between the male
and female lovers.[1] The female often speaks and initiates
loving action. The male is often gentle and coy. And both
male and female have beauty and sensuality. There is no
stereotyping of gender here, and this fits in perfectly with the
biblical understanding of the mutuality of husband and wife
in Gen 2.

Similarly, this mutuality accords with modern marital
counseling. It has been pointed out that there can be no
satisfactory marital life apart from the achievement of shared
power between wife and husband (cf. Eph 5:21). Spouses
must resolve the issue of how to make decisions together, and
they must learn to resolve disagreements in a way that is
satisfactory to both partners. The power of final decisions
shifts back and forth between spouses. Each spouse sometimes exercises authority, in oneness and respect for the
other. And of course that finally is the gift that Christ has
given to marital love. For, as Paul writes, in Christ, "there is
neither male nor female; for all of you are one in Christ Jesus"
(Gal 3:18). In him, the ancient war between the sexes has
been stilled, and the joyful unity of one flesh in marriage has
become possible again. Human love between male and female, in the love of Christ, is indeed a wondrous gift of a
loving God!

Notes

1. This was pointed out to me by Marcia Falk in her commentary on the Song of Songs in *Harper's Bible Commentary*, 528.

PART THREE

Prophets and Lamentations

❧ 21 ❧

"Streams in the Desert"

ISAIAH 35:1–10

*N*OT ONLY THE TEXTS THAT DEAL WITH GOD'S JUDG-
ment give us difficulty. Very often we are at a loss as to
how to preach the Old Testament texts that picture, in
fantastic terms, God's future salvation of his people. This is
an Advent text that pictures the future blessedness of the
new age of salvation, but its specificities may give us hermeneutical problems.

Plumbing the Text

The passage follows the judgment on the nations in Isa
34 and, by way of contrast, portrays the salvation of Judah.
The two chapters together form the transition between the
first Isaiah (chs. 1–39) and the second (chs. 40–55), echoing
themes from both.[1]

So closely related is Isa 35:1–10 to Second Isaiah (Isa
40–55) that it has often been thought to come from that
author. The return of the redeemed and ransomed to Zion
(vv. 9–10) is similar to Isa 51:10–11. The revelation of the glory
of the Lord (v. 2) reminds the reader of Isa 40:5. The fertile
flourishing of the wilderness is common in Second Isaiah
(41:18–19; 43:19–20; 51:3, etc.). Blindness and deafness (v. 5)
characterize Israel in Isa 42:18–19. (But that characterization
is given also in Isa 6:9–10.)

The historical context of the text differs somewhat from that of Second Isaiah, however. The latter book sounds its universal, eschatological theme out of the specific context of the Babylonian exile and the return from that captivity. Isaiah 35, on the other hand, has the whole Jewish diaspora in mind. God's judgment in Isa 34 and his salvation of his people in Isa 35 encompass all nations and all the dispersed of the covenant people. The Babylonian exile is not specified and lies in the past. Thus, Isa 34 and 35 were probably added later by an editor as a way of joining the first and the second Isaiahs.

What are the specific themes of this text? The first theme is the transformation of the desert wilderness into abundant fertility. Second is the revelation of the glory of the Lord, coming to recompense his people for their suffering and to save them. The third theme is the command to the people, therefore, to be strong and not to fear. Fourth is the healing of the blind and deaf, the lame and dumb, and fifth is the return of the redeemed, ransomed people of God to Zion on a Holy Way, unhindered by either historical or natural foes. Finally there is the theme of the bestowal of everlasting joy to the people, who will be free of all sorrow and sighing.

The emphasis of the text is therefore on the coming of the Lord to save his people and the marvelous results of that coming. Everything is changed because the Lord comes to save.

Forming the Sermon

We are dealing in this text with eschatology, with the future coming of the new age of God's kingdom on earth. But the consistent testimony of the New Testament is that the Kingdom of God began to break into human history in the person and deeds of Jesus Christ. The coming of the fullness of the kingdom awaits Christ's return. But its powers and conditions began to be present when Jesus started his ministry. "The time is fulfilled," was his first announcement, "and the kingdom of God is at hand" (Mark 1:15).

The marks of that kingdom, therefore, were present in Jesus' ministry. "Go and tell John [the Baptist] what you hear and see," Jesus told John's inquiring disciples. "The blind receive their sight and the lame walk, lepers are cleansed and the deaf hear, and the dead are raised up, and the poor have good news preached to them" (Matt 11:4–5). Jesus pointed to the fulfillment in his works of Isa 35:5–6 and other portions of the Isaiah tradition (Isa 29:18–19; 61:1). The new age of God began to come on this earth when Jesus Christ walked among us, and so all of history is now divided into B.C., before Christ, and A.D., anno domini, the year of our Lord, the new age of God.

We have no difficulty announcing during Advent that we are waiting for the birth of the One who fulfills portions of this prophecy. And Isaiah's announcement of the coming of the Lord and of the revelation of his glory fits right in with our Advent expectations. But what do we do with the rest of this text of Isa 35? What do we do with the promise of streams in the desert? Nothing in our natural world is changed by the coming of Christ at Christmastime.

The images of this text yield their meaning when we realize that the "wilderness" and "desert" in Second Isaiah and in this passage are symbols for these prophets of life without God. The old age, without God in our lives, is like a desert, says our text. It is the age of desolation, of thirst, of wandering aimlessly through the wilderness of life. Or, in the words of T. S. Eliot, the old age is a wasteland:

> A heap of broken images, where the sun beats,
> And the dead tree gives no shelter, the cricket no relief,
> And the dry stone no sound of water.[2]

The old age is a time of despair, of no hope in the world— where generation after generation of young men go to war's bloody graves with no good result from their sacrifice; a time when the strong strut ruthlessly through the earth and the weak have no helper; an age when violence rules a city's streets and the dark is a place of terror; an age when hatreds fester in our living rooms and families fall apart. The old age is a time without God, when fulfillment lies only in ourselves; a time when pride drives us to a life of constant competition with our colleagues; a time when there is no ultimate meaning to all that we are doing, and work after all is just a way to

125

make a buck. The ruler of the old age is the specter death, and all through the course of it, he inexorably claims his victims, putting an end to every dream, every joy, every lovely human relationship.

The glad news of Isa 35:1–10, then, is that there will come a new age, and the New Testament proclaims that it has begun in Jesus Christ. If we use the images of our text, then we can say that the new age is no longer a time of desert, of aimless wandering through the wilderness. Rather, it is a time of well-watered abundance, a time when flowers bloom in the crannies of human lives and bent souls are straightened and given some majesty. It is a time when sorrow and sighing have been done away, and joyful song has broken the stillness. It is a time when the powers of death no longer reign on the earth, and human beings are ransomed from the evil forces that hold them captive—from fear, from sin, from anxiety and weakness, from meaningless wandering through their days. Human life, with all its still, sad song of sorrow, will be transformed into praise and joy, into wholeness and health. And that new age, with its wondrous powers, began to come in Jesus Christ, whose birth we celebrate at Christmastime.[3] God comes to save us, as our text announces, in the person of his Son.

In some such manner the images of this Isaiah text can yield their joyous meaning.

Notes

1. Most scholars now agree that the book of Isaiah is made up of the oracles of three different prophets or prophetic groups: Isaiah, chs. 1–39, from the eighth century B.C.; Second Isaiah, chs. 40–55, from the Babylonian exile, ca. 550–538 B.C.; and Third Isaiah, chs. 56–66, from ca. 538–500 B.C., after the return from exile.

2. *The Waste Land,* Part I. "The Burial of the Dead," lines 22–24.

3. These thoughts on the characteristics of the old and new ages are taken from my sermon, entitled "B.C. and A.D.," which was published in my book, *Nature, God, and Pulpit* (Grand Rapids: Eerdmans, 1992), 174–215.

❧ 22 ❧

"I Make
Weal and Create Woe"

ISAIAH 45:1–7

Plumbing the Text

THESE SEVEN VERSES CONSTITUTE THE SECOND STANZA OR
strophe of a longer three-strophe poem in Isa 44:24–45:13.
They are a portion of the book that is known as Second Isaiah,
which includes chs. 40–55 in the Book of Isaiah, and which
was prophesied to the Israelite exiles in Babylonia between
550 and 538 B.C.

The text reflects the history of the time. From 605 to
550 B.C., the Babylonian Empire dominated the countries of
the ancient Near East. However, in 550 B.C. Cyrus II of Persia
rose to power and, after assuming control over Media and
Lydia, conquered Babylon in 539 B.C. In 538, he issued a
decree that allowed the Jews in Babylonia to return to Palestine under the leadership of the Davidic Sheshbazzar. At the
same time, Cyrus ordered that the temple in Jerusalem should
be rebuilt at Persian expense and its sacred vessels returned
to it (Ezra 1:2–4, 7–11; 6:3–5).

Second Isaiah as a whole therefore reflects both its
historical background and the wider eschatological promises
of God. It deals with the promise of return of the exiles to
Jerusalem, but it also envisions the eschatological future
when "all flesh shall see the glory of the LORD" (40:5) and

"every knee shall bow" and "every tongue shall swear" that
the Lord alone is God (45:23). Our particular text centers on
the historical rise of Cyrus to power and his freeing decrees.

The seven verses of the poem in Isa 45:1–7 are emphatic
in their assertion of God's lordship. "I am the LORD" occurs
four times (vv. 3, 5, 6, 7; cf. 44:24). God is the absolute Lord
over historical events, the only God, besides whom there is
no other. In the first strophe of 44:24–27, his lordship over
the cosmos is asserted (vv. 24, 27) and his power to fulfill his
purposes is set forth (v. 26). Now in this second strophe,
God's lordship over empires is given concrete example. God
can summon the great Cyrus of Persia to carry out his historical purpose for Israel (cf. 44:28).

In 44:28, Cyrus was called the Lord's "shepherd." Now
in 45:1, he is named God's "anointed," God's *mashiah*. That
is the Hebrew word from which we get our word Messiah,
and that is a startling designation for a foreign king; no non-
Israelite is ever given the name. However, the title here does
not bear the full messianic meaning found in other prophetic
writings and in the New Testament. There are a few texts in
which the word is applied to the prophets generally (Ps
105=1 Chron 16:22) or to Israel (Hab 3:13). As it is used
here, it indicates that Cyrus has been consecrated as the
instrument of the Lord's purpose. God has grasped Cyrus'
hand (v. 1), an indication of God's protection of him (cf.
41:13; 42:6). And God will subdue nations before him and
make other kings powerless, which is the meaning of "ungird
the loins of kings," v. 1.

But we should mark carefully that it is God who will
defeat Cyrus' opponents, giving him the power to conquer.
Note the three-fold repetition of "I" in vv. 2 and 3. God will
go before the armies of Cyrus. God will break down enemy
defenses and give Cyrus the vast treasures of Babylonia.
Ultimately, nations have no power unless they are empowered
by God.

God will give Cyrus victories, however, all for the sake
of his servant and chosen people Israel, v. 4. God has a
purpose that he is carrying out through Israel—the purpose

128

of using her to be his witnesses to all peoples that he alone is God (43:10, 12; 44:8). Second Isaiah asserts that when the nations see God's salvation of his people Israel, they will learn and know that the Lord alone is God and there is no other (vv. 4, 5; such is the import too of Isa 52:13–53:12).

Cyrus does not know that he is an instrument in the hands of the Lord (vv. 4, 5). God surnames him—that is, gives him an honorary title (perhaps "anointed")—and girds him with strength for war (vv. 4–5). God can use human nations and rulers as his instruments, and he often does so (cf. Isa 10:5), while they are unaware of his rule. But God is the one Lord, whose sovereignty rules all nature and history, who creates light and darkness in the realm of nature, and who sends weal and creates woe in the sphere of history (v. 7).

Forming the Sermon

Verse 7 of our text bothers many people. How, they ask, can it be said that God creates woe? Is God not wholly good, a God who would never send woe on anyone? After all, we have in the first chapter of Genesis the affirmation that God made his creation "very good" (Gen 1:31), and it follows therefore that if there is evil in the world it did not come from the hand of God. Yet this verse in Second Isaiah seems to contradict that revelation.

Further, even in the midst of tragedy—such as when a child dies or a natural catastrophe strikes—the church assures us that God is nevertheless good. God wills only good for us. God wants it to go well with us (cf. Deut 5:29). He sent his Son that we might have life and have it abundantly (John 10:10). Surely he wouldn't create woe in our lives.

Further still, God works in many ways to bring good out of our evil. The story of Joseph in Genesis explicitly sets forth that working (Gen 50:20). And Paul tells us that "in everything God works for good with those who love him, who are called according to his purpose" (Rom 8:28). Would God, then, "create woe?" This verse in Second Isaiah's writings seems to contradict everything we have believed about God.

We have such difficulty with this text, because—as with so many verses in the Bible—we lift it out of its context. Instead of understanding it in its historical setting, we extract the verse as a general principle about the nature of God. But God is speaking to Cyrus of Persia here. He is telling Cyrus that he will defeat Cyrus' enemies before him, and that in fact will mean "woe" for those enemies. The verse is simply another affirmation of the sovereignty of God over all nations.

The Bible is quite sure that God sometimes exercises lordship over the proud or evil nations and brings "woe" upon them. The prophet Jeremiah, for example, in his call, is set over nations not only "to build and to plant," but also to "pluck up and to break down, to destroy and to overthrow" (Jer 1:10). Isaiah of Jerusalem utters a devastating taunt song against the king of Babylonia, who has said in his pride and ruthlessness, "I will ascend above the heights of the clouds, I will make myself like the Most High" (Isa 14:14). Human rulers cannot claim that they are God and get away with it. And Second Isaiah himself tells us that the Lord "brings princes to nought, and makes the rulers of the earth as nothing" (Isa 40:23).

> Scarcely are they planted, scarcely sown,
>   scarcely has their stem taken root in the earth,
> when he blows upon them, and they wither,
>   and the tempest carries them off like stubble. (Isa 40:24)

In our world where so many think we are at the mercy of national and international governments, terrorists, military, and multinational corporations, this is very good news. God is in control of the powers and principalities and can bring "woe" upon them.

The third strophe of Isa 44:24–45:13 also picks up the "woe" of v. 7, as well as the verb "make" from that verse. There, in 45:9–10, "woe" is pronounced upon those who strive against their Maker or who question his will for the people he has made. That brings v. 7 down to a personal level, although the strophe is actually still concerned with God's work through Cyrus. But "woe to him who strives with his Maker" (v. 9).

Is that not also a comforting thought, that those who defy the will of God cannot ultimately succeed, but trouble and finally death will come upon them? The entire New Testament sets forth that thought, that life and good are finally to be had through faith in Jesus Christ alone, and that those who turn against him cannot win the victory. God does bring "woe" upon his enemies. God does judge people for their wrong, because God does indeed will only good for his earth and not evil. Therefore we have the assurance that the violence, the corruption, the sin that we see all around us in our society is not the last word. Rather, God's good will prevail, and the kingdom of good will come on earth as it already is in heaven.

That does not mean, of course, that even the faithful will not suffer distress and woe. Human sin has its consequences, and we suffer not only the woeful outworkings of our own sin, but also those of the society and world around us.

But is woe for us finally, then, what we can expect from God for what we do? After all, none of us is perfectly faithful, none perfectly good and holy, none wholly a friend of our Lord Jesus Christ. Nevertheless, he died on the cross to forgive our sins and he rose triumphant over them. And he has promised us that if in faith we trust him, knowing we have no righteousness in ourselves, we will inherit life eternal in his kingdom of good. All of us must finally pray, "God, be merciful to me a sinner" (Luke 18:13). And God in Christ hears that prayer, and grants his overflowing, abundant mercy.

❧ 23 ❧

"Thou Didst Pierce the Dragon"

ISAIAH 51:9–11

WHETHER OR NOT THIS TEXT IS EVER USED AS THE basis for a sermon—and it could be used with profit—it contains a concept that is used so widely throughout both Old and New Testaments, and that is so important for understanding many other biblical passages, that I have chosen to deal with it here. I refer to the lines that speak of God cutting Rahab in pieces and piercing the dragon. Few congregations have any inkling as to what that means.

Plumbing the Text

Isaiah 51:9–11 is spoken by Second Isaiah[1] himself, and these verses constitute a brief imperative in which the prophet speaks for the people in Babylonian exile, summoning the Lord to come to their aid. The exiles believe that God is asleep and needs to be wakened (cf. Ps 44:23; 78:65). But as following passages indicate, it is the exiles who need to be roused (Isa 51:17; 52:1), and vv. 9–11 are really intended as announcements of salvation to the exiles, as are all of the poems in the immediate context.

The text refers to three events in the history of God's dealings with Israel. Verses 9–10b refer to God's creation of the world, v. 10cd refers to the exodus from Egypt, and v. 11 pictures the final eschatological salvation, when exiled Israel will return to Zion. Thus, the creation and exodus form the theological basis on which Israel is to rest its hope for the future.

We are principally concerned in this essay with the view of God's creation of the world in vv. 9–10b. Who is Rahab, and what does it mean that God pierced the dragon? This is what needs to be explained for a modern congregation.

Genesis 1 tells us that in the beginning, the earth was without form and void *(tohu wabohu)*. There was nothing but chaos, and that chaos is pictured in the symbol of water, called the "deep." Over the face of the waters moved the wind of God,[2] so that the picture is one of stormy, raging waters in darkness. God's act of creation in Gen 1 consists, therefore, in bringing light and order into the chaos, so that life becomes possible (cf. Isa 45:18–19).

God creates the order that makes life possible by pushing back the chaos and giving it bounds. Light is created and separated from darkness (Gen 1:3–5). The solid arc of the firmament is raised up and holds some of the waters in check above the firmament, while the rest of the waters below are parted and held captive below the earth, so that the dry land of earth can appear (Gen 1:6–10). With the waters of chaos thus held back and bounded by his Word, God can proceed to create all of the life that we find in our universe. To be sure, the waters of chaos are still there, but they are held in check by the faithfulness and power of God (cf. Job 38:8–11; Ps 104:5–9).

In short, the very structure of our universe, the Old Testament is saying, is dependent on the faithfulness of God. If God did not have control over the chaos, the universe would return to its unformed, chaotic state. Only once did that happen, says Genesis, when God allowed the waters of the "great deep" to pour forth in the flood in the time of Noah (Gen 7:11). But after the flood, God's promise to Noah was that he would never again let the waters of chaos cover the earth (Gen 9:8–17). Jeremiah ominously warns, however, that

God's final judgment on our sin might consist in allowing chaos *(tohu wabohu)* to return (Jer 4:23–26).

In accordance with language that was used in the ancient Near East, the chaos has other names in the Old Testament. Sometimes it is called "Rahab" or "the dragon" or "Leviathan." The cultures of Mesopotamia, for example, portrayed chaos in the figure of a dragon that had to be slain by the gods. Our text here in Isa 51 is borrowing that language (as also in Ps 74:13–14; 89:9–10). In his creation of the universe, God slew the dragon Rahab, by which is meant, God defeated the waters of chaos and now keeps them from breaking loose. And that act of creation is made parallel in our text, then, to God's driving back the waters of the Reed Sea so as to allow Israel to pass through on dry land in its exodus from Egypt.

It should also be noted that frequently throughout both Testaments the chaotic waters are meant when simply the word "sea" is used. For example, Ps 46:1–3 speaks of the "sea," whose waters "roar and foam" so that the mountains "tremble with its tumult." The Psalmist is referring to much more than just the ordinary ocean. That is chaos that threatens Israel, but God is the congregation's "refuge and strength." Or in the story of Jesus calming the storm in Mark 4:35–41, the miracle is not simply that Jesus calms a storm on the sea of Galilee. Rather, that which inspires the disciples' awe is that the "sea" obeys him. The story is pointing to Jesus' identity, for it is only the Creator God who can control the sea, the chaos.

Throughout the Scriptures, we find the picture of chaos that is always associated with evil, darkness, and death. But opposed to chaos are God's order and goodness, God's light and life. And it is in God alone that we may find our salvation from chaos's evil, disordered, dark death.

Forming the Sermon

Israel knew that she lived always on the fringe of chaos— or at least those who authored the Old Testament knew that.

Life, said the Israelites, was always threatened by death, as so many of the Psalmists attest. Evil lurked at the edges of every community and could undermine its good, as the prophets continually saw. Disorder could invade the monarchy, as it often did, and darkness rather than the light of understanding and insight could characterize every thought. As a result, the Old Testament's witnesses proclaimed that life and light, order and good were to be had in God alone, for he alone was Ruler over the chaos (cf. Ps 29:10). He had defeated it in the beginning at creation, and his faithfulness was constantly preventing its deadly powers from invading Israel's life. The waters of chaos could roar and foam and the mountains tremble with the tumult, but Israel needed to have no fear because God was her refuge and strength (Ps 46).

Chaos creeps around the edges of our lives too, does it not? We know very well what it means when Job says that Leviathan can be roused, for we continually see the beast of chaos threatening our life's territory. Out on the fringes of every quiet suburb or town there is a drug war going on. Circling around every marriage are the threats of indifference, unfaithfulness, dispute. Haunting every doctor's visit is that fear of cancer, heart disease, termination. Threatening every one of our children is the lure of a society gone crazy with sex. Oh yes, we live daily with the threat of chaos and at night, it sometimes overwhelms our dreams. And so we need to listen very carefully to what our prophet tells his people.

God is in control of the chaos, Second Isaiah proclaims. God defeated it when he made our world and put chains and bars around its powers (see Job 38:8–10 for the figure). He ruled over chaos when he led his people on dry land out of Egypt and delivered them from the powers of evil's slavery and injustice. And now, all you people who are threatened by darkness, disorder, evil, and death can still find your refuge and strength in God. The waters will not overwhelm you, and when you walk through fire you will not be burned. "For I am the LORD your God, the Holy One of Israel, your Savior" (Isa 43:3).

But more than that, good Christians, the Scriptures tell us that there will come a day when chaos and evil will be done away forever. Our text pictures that final day when exiled Israel will return to Zion with singing, and everlasting joy shall be upon their heads. But other texts in Old and New Testaments tell of that day also. "In that day," proclaims an earlier Isaiah, "the LORD with his hard and great and strong sword will punish Leviathan the fleeing serpent, Leviathan the twisting serpent, and he will slay the dragon that is in the seas" (Isa 27:1).

And so the New Testament, in its picture of the Kingdom of God come on earth, tells us that John of Patmos saw in a vision a new heaven and a new earth, coming down out of heaven from God, and that in that kingdom there was no more chaotic evil, for "the sea—the chaos—was no more" (Rev 21:1-2). God himself will be with us, John wrote. He will wipe away every tear from our eyes, and death shall be no more, neither shall there be mourning nor crying nor pain any more, for the former things will have passed away (Rev 21:3-4). Chaos will be gone. God will be the Ruler over all. That is the future for every true Christian.

Notes

1. See ch. 21, n. 1, on Second Isaiah.
2. The word for wind should not be read here as "Spirit," even though many modern interpretations picture the Spirit of God as the instrument of God's creation of the world. God does not create by his Spirit, however, but by his Word, and "wind" is a better rendering, giving simply a picture of stormy waters.

136

❦ 24 ❧

Strange Prophetic Actions

JEREMIAH 13:1–11

*T*HROUGHOUT THE STORIES AND WRITINGS OF THE prophets, we find them performing strange actions that we would attribute to mental illness were they done in our day. For example, the early prophet Ahijah takes off the robe he is wearing, tears it into twelve pieces and gives ten of the pieces to Jeroboam, symbolizing the division of Solomon's former kingdom into two realms, under Rehoboam in the south and Jeroboam in the north (1 Kgs 11:29–38). Isaiah walks for three years naked and barefoot in Jerusalem, as a sign of the captivity of Egypt and Ethiopia to Assyria (Isa 20:1–6). Jeremiah is commanded to buy an earthenware pot and to break and bury it in the valley of Topheth, as a sign of the destruction and defiling of Judah and Jerusalem (Jer 19:1–13). Similarly, Jeremiah is told by the Lord to wear a wooden yoke to symbolize that Judah will fall under the yoke of Babylonia (Jer 27:1–11). When the rival prophet Hananiah removes the wooden yoke from Jeremiah's shoulders, Jeremiah replaces it with an iron yoke (Jer 28).

Most bizarre of all, however, are the actions carried out by the prophet Ezekiel. He draws an outline of Jerusalem on a clay brick and constructs little siege works around it. He eats meager food, cooked over cow's dung, and rations his water (Ezek 4). He shaves his head and divides the hair into three portions, burning the first, striking the second with a sword, and scattering the third to the wind (Ezek 5:1–2). He packs up his baggage and sets it outside his house in daylight. Then at night, he breaks through the wall of his house and leaves furtively (Ezek 12:1–7). All these strange actions point toward the siege and destruction of Jerusalem by the armies of the Babylonian Empire in 587 B.C.

These sorts of actions are known as "prophetic symbolic actions," and because the prophets perform them so frequently, it is necessary to know how to interpret them.

Plumbing the Text

In the first seven verses of Jer 13, the prophet is commanded by the Lord to buy a linen undergarment and to put it on. Then God commands him to take off the undergarment, to take it to the Euphrates River, and to hide it there in a cleft in the rock. After a lengthy period of time, Jeremiah is then commanded to retrieve the undergarment and to see that it is rotted and spoiled. In vv. 8–11, the Lord interprets the action for the prophet. As the undergarment has been spoiled, so God will spoil the pride of Jerusalem and Judah, for their people's idolatry.

That such prophetic actions are not audio-visual aids to the prophetic preaching is clear from this text. No audience observes the prophetic action here. Thus, it has its meaning apart from any observers. The fact that Jeremiah is commanded to go to the Euphrates, which would be a distance of seven hundred miles, makes the literal interpretation improbable. Probably what we have here is a report of a vision of the prophet's, in which he travels to the Euphrates in a vision, just as Ezekiel travels in a vision from Babylon to Jerusalem (Ezek 8:3). But Jeremiah probably did actually bury and then later dig up the loincloth in a place that for him stood for the Euphrates. The word of the Lord that emerges out of the action and vision is clear, however. God is going to spoil Judah and Jerusalem by means of their destruction and exile to Babylonia.

Forming the Sermon

The God of the Bible is not a God who just speaks words. He is also a God who acts. When God determines to exercise his judgment upon his covenant people for their unfaithfulness to him, he does not merely utter words of condemnation, which the people may hear or refuse to hear (cf. Ezek 3:11). No. God acts, and the beginning of that action is found in these prophetic symbolic actions. They do not merely predict the future; they begin it. They start an action of God's that will not cease until the judgment is complete and Judah and Jerusalem are in fact spoiled.

Actually, we could say the same thing about the Word of God—that it begins an action. Throughout the Bible, that Word does not merely convey information. Rather, the Word of God works. It is effective, powerful force that shapes events and brings about that of which it speaks (cf. Isa 55:10–11; Ezek 12:26–28). So when God speaks to us, he is not just telling us something. He is acting in our lives. God says, "Your sins are forgiven," and that Word acts actually to forgive us and to restore us to fellowship with the Father. God says, "Peace I leave with you," and God begins to create peace within our hearts. It is for this reason that we sometimes feel ourselves so moved and transformed when we hear the words of Scripture. They are words that create in us that of which they tell.

But here in our Jeremiah text, God begins the action of judgment against his sinful people through the means of the symbolic action of his prophet. And that action, and others like it, begin the events that will in fact lead to Judah's downfall. That which we should notice most carefully perhaps are the reasons why God will destroy his covenant people, for we too in the church are the covenant people of God through Christ.

God had made Israel and Judah nations that were to cling to him. The word "cling" is deliberately chosen. God's people were to be as close to him as a loincloth is to a man. Their relationship was not one of legalistic obedience or

139

ritual correctness. Israel was made to be related to God in an intimate communion, like that of a faithful wife with her husband, or like that of an adoring son with his father (cf. Jer 3:19–20; 31:20). God set his heart in love upon Israel (Deut 10:15), and Israel was to cleave in her heart to God (Deut 10:20), to love him with all her heart and soul and might (Deut 6:4). It was to be the same relationship that we today are to have with our God through Christ (Mark 12:30).

In such a relationship, says our text, Israel would then be God's people, whose life and well-being would bring others to praise his name and to give him glory (Jer 13:11). Our Lord Jesus pointed to the same result of our love and service of God (Matt 5:16).

Israel, however, rejected God's love and closed her heart to him, like a wife rejecting all her husband's care and affection. She sought out other lovers, other gods, and instead worshiped at their shrines and did whatever her wanton heart pleased. Our text calls that self-will "pride," because it substitutes human will for God's. So God's judgment on Israel was entirely just, sending her into exile. She had spoiled her life with God, and she would suffer the result of that spoilage.

Despite the large emphasis this text has on judgment, I think perhaps the most important thing it gives us is the picture of that garment clinging to the prophet. It is such a powerful symbol of God's clinging to us and of us clinging to him in turn. Using an idiom of our day, maybe we should say that we are to know our God, through the Scriptures and through prayer, as well as we know the inside of our shirt—to be so intimately related to him, through all our daily walk, that we cannot be separated from his love that clings as closely to us as does our clothing. And then to pray, and pray every day, that we do not shed his love by our actions and thus become rotten and spoiled. God has clothed us with the garment of his pure love and goodness through Christ. Cling to that clothing and wrap it securely round you!

❧ 25 ❧

Mourning

LAMENTATIONS 1:1–6

*T*HIS IS THE STATED OLD TESTAMENT READING FOR THE twenty-seventh Sunday in Pentecost or Ordinary Time in Cycle C of the three-year lectionary. Its use from the pulpit can furnish the church the opportunity to do that which has long been ignored in our modern worship services—the opportunity to mourn.

Plumbing the Text

The Book of Lamentations is made up of five long poems in acrostic form. That is, each verse in the poem begins with one of the twenty-two letters of the Hebrew alphabet, proceeding in order. Thus the first poem in ch. 1, for which our text forms the beginning, has twenty-two verses, running from the Hebrew *aleph* to *taw*, and our particular text covers the first six letters of the alphabet. We might say that the subjects are being covered from A to Z.

All of the poems are laments over the destruction of Jerusalem by the armies of Babylonia in 587 B.C. At that time, all but the poorest peasants in Jerusalem were carried into exile in Babylonia. However, those left behind in the city carried on some form of worship in the ruins of the temple on Mt. Zion (cf. Jer 41:5), and it is very likely that the poems of Lamentations were used in that worship. Much later, after the rebuilt temple was destroyed by the Romans in A.D. 70, these laments were read annually in the commemoration of the temple's loss that was held on the ninth of the month of Ab (July-August).

Probably the book was compiled during the sixth century B.C. It was traditionally connected with the prophet Jeremiah, partly on the basis of 2 Chron 35:25, contributing to the popular but erroneous view of Jeremiah as a weeping and sorrowful prophet.

Lamentations shares the prophetic view that the fall of Judah and destruction of Jerusalem were God's punishment of his faithless people for their idolatry and rebellion against his lordship. In fact, there is even the passing thought that the judgment on Israel was part of the Day of the Lord (1:12, 21; see my discussion of that concept in connection with Zephaniah in ch. 31). Throughout the book, therefore, there are prominent confessions of sin and pleas for God's mercy. But there are also expressions of faith in God's steadfast love and salvation (cf. 3:22–27). The latter, however, do not occur in our brief text.

Our text of Lam 1:1–6 opens with a funeral lament over Jerusalem that is portrayed in the figure of a woman who has lost her husband (v. 1). She who was great among the nations and even called a princess has now become a vassal slave to Babylonia. She has been betrayed by all of her allies and friends, with no one to comfort her (vv. 1, 19). She who was God's special people, "not reckoning itself among the nations" (Num 23:9), has become like every other conquered nation of the ancient Near East (v. 3). Even her roads to Zion are pictured as mourning, because the annual pilgrimages to Zion for the feasts of Tabernacles, Passover, and Weeks have ceased (v. 4). Her children, that is, her population, have been taken from her into exile (vv. 1, 5). Her leaders are gone—most of them deported in the first exile of 597 B.C. There is a scarcity of food, as there always is in any conquered nation (vv. 11, 19) And worst of all perhaps, her foes now gloat over her downfall (vv. 7, 21).

Some of the Psalms picture the anguish of Israel over the destruction of Zion and the taunt of their foes.

O God, the heathen have come into thy inheritance;
  they have defiled thy holy temple;
  they have laid Jerusalem in ruins.

. . .

We have become a taunt to our neighbors,
  mocked and derided by those round about us.

. . .

Why should the nations say,
  "Where is their God?" (Ps 79:1, 4, 10; cf. Ps 115:1–2)

It is precisely because of Israel's failure to worship and
serve the Lord alone, however, that she finds herself in such
a situation of distress, and this is confessed in our poem.

Her foes have become the head,
  her enemies prosper,
because the LORD has made her suffer
  for the multitude of her transgressions. (Lam 1:5)

Israel's fall to Babylonia has not been simply an event in
secular history that would have occurred anyway. Rather it has
been the direct result of God's working in human affairs to
deliver his people into the hands of the Babylonians. Indeed,
there is no sense in the Bible of what we would call "secular"
or "ordinary" history. The affairs of persons and nations are
under the control of the Lord of history and through the events
of human lives, God works out his purpose. The prophet
Jeremiah knew that, and so he even urged besieged Jerusalem
to surrender to the Babylonian armies, because he knew that
Babylonia was being used as an instrument in the hands of God
(cf. Jer 32:1–6). It was also revealed to him, however, as it was
to Second Isaiah (cf. Isa 40:1–2), that Israel's exile would come
to an end and that God, in his mercy, had for his chosen people
"a future and a hope" (Jer 29:10–11). Lamentations shares the
same abiding faith (Lam 3:21–27).

Forming the Sermon

It may be that the preacher will want to use this text to
speak of God's lordship over history. Perhaps more than any

143

other learning, we modern-day Christians need to become aware of God's relation to every event that takes place. This is the unique focus of the entire Bible, that God is its main subject, and that all of the affairs of history and nature are related to his working toward his goal of bringing in his kingdom on earth. To be conscious of the presence of God in every event, to have a world-view that is saturated with the knowledge, gained from the Scriptures, of the Lord's rule—that is true spirituality. For our purposes in this book, however, I want to take a different approach to this text from Lamentations.

It was the fad some years ago in the church to speak of worship as "celebration." Certainly it is that. We praise our God, celebrating his mighty deeds of mercy on our behalf.

But it is a characteristic of biblical worship, typified in the Psalms and here in Lamentations, that worship of God has two poles—praise and lament. Indeed, two-thirds of the Psalms are laments, and the canon has included this whole book of laments of Lamentations.

We think of lamenting and mourning only in relation to a death, and even then we sometimes hurry past the grief with assurances that "it was for the best" or "time heals all wounds" or "it was God's will" or "things will work out all right." Psychologically, we do not dwell on mourning and lamenting. In fact, we often shun the mourner, because we do not know what to say, or their mourning reminds us of our own vulnerability. But people need time to mourn, and we know that if mourning does not take place at the time of a death, it will surface sooner or later.

However, death is not the only occasion when persons lament. I participated in a forum about the victims of crime some time ago, and we heard that crime victims need a time to mourn—to recount their experience, to surface their emotions, and to lament their loss of property or health or security and selfhood. Other people need time to mourn the breakup of a relationship, or the loss of employment, a shattering of dreams, or a loss of skills. Some lament when a friend has a tragedy or a loved one moves far away. And surely many know the laments that go with loneliness, with anxiety in the night, and with fear and loss of hope for the future.

Our passage in Lamentations attributes its mourning to the destruction of war. How many in our world suffer that! But finally, Lamentations mourns the results of transgressions against God and the resulting loss of God's favor. Lament turns into confession, therefore, and confession brings new hope in the passages that follow our particular text.

The only notice we take of such laments in our worship is evidenced in the congregation's confession of sin. But sometimes even that is omitted by a people who shun the thought of sin. In a society that is rapidly losing all sense of ultimate right and wrong, sin and the mourning for its results are given very short shrift, overlooking the fact that most of our troubles and afflictions in the world are in fact the results of our sin.

So perhaps this passage from Lamentations can remind us that we are indeed suffering because of sin. And perhaps readings from Lamentations, along with the Psalms of Lament, can give voice to the sorrow that is in us, can bind us together with our fellow worshipers who are suffering also, and can lead to a heartfelt confession to God and finally to his assurance of mercy. "Blessed are those who mourn, for they shall be comforted" (Matt 5:4). Lament allowed can lead to true repentance and a new relationship to the God, whose mercies are new every morning (Lam 3:22).

❧ 26 ❧

God in Human Form?

EZEKIEL 1:26–28

Plumbing the Text

THE PROPHET EZEKIEL, WHO CAME FROM A ZADOKITE
priestly family and who may initially have been a priest
himself, did not begin his prophetic ministry until after he
was exiled to Babylonia, along with the leaders and upper-
class citizens of Judah, in the first deportation of 597 B.C.
While he was with a group of the exiles who had been settled
beside the Chebar Canal near the central Babylonian city
of Nippur, Ezekiel reports that on July 1, 593 B.C., "the
heavens were opened, and I saw visions of God" (1:1). As 1:3
states, "the hand of the LORD was upon him," which is
probably indicative of an ecstatic prophetic experience (cf.
1 Kgs 18:46).

In his ecstatic vision, Ezekiel was given to see a glowing
storm cloud, with fire flashing forth from its midst. Emerging
from the fire there came four living creatures, who had something like human forms, but each had four faces, four wings
with human hands under them, and bovine hoofs. Beneath
the four creatures that shone like burnished bronze, there
were wheels, set at right angles with one another, so that the
four creatures could move in any direction. On the wheels
were eyes that could see anywhere, and above the four creatures there was a crystalline expanse, called a firmament.

Above the firmament was something like a sapphire throne, and on the throne there was something like the likeness of a human form, gleaming like bronze, with fire and brightness round about him. This was, writes Ezekiel, "the appearance of the likeness of the glory of the LORD,"—a vision of the Lord in the shining, transcendent effulgence of his glory. "And," records the prophet, "when I saw it, I fell upon my face, and I heard the voice of one speaking" (v. 28). Such was the vision that introduced Ezekiel's call to a prophetic ministry. "Son of man," the Lord said to him, "I send you to the people of Israel, to a nation of rebels" (2:3), "and you shall speak my words to them, whether they hear or refuse to hear; for they are a rebellious house" (2:7).

In this vision and call of Ezekiel there are several features that we wish to note. First, the bizarre images of the vision strain to describe what cannot be described—the heavenly creatures propelling the throne-chariot of the Lord God, who sees and goes through all the earth, and whose glory transcends all human understandings.

Second, this vision appears to the prophet in the alien land of Babylonia. Prophecy was not supposed to take place outside of Israel, but the vision Ezekiel is given breaks all human boundaries and brings God's words to those who have been punished for their sin by being exiled to Babylonia, as well as to those inhabitants who remain still in Jerusalem. The exiles' way was not "hid from the LORD," as they had complained (Isa 40:27). They were to seek and to pray to the Lord even in Babylonia (Jer 29:7).

Third, Ezekiel was to speak the Word of the Lord to the Israelites whether they heard or refused to hear. In short, Ezek 1:26–28 displays the power and effectiveness of the Word of God which, once released by a prophet, works in human life and brings about events, until what the Word has said is fulfilled (cf. Isa 55:10–11; Ezek 12:28). We can accept God's Word or reject it, but the Word will accomplish that of which it speaks. Thus, the judgments on Jerusalem that Ezekiel proclaims in chs. 3–24 of his book will be realized in the fall of Jerusalem to the Babylonians in 587 B.C. But

147

equally, the words of salvation that Ezekiel pronounces in chs. 34–39[1] will also be fulfilled by God.

Fourth, and most important for our particular concern, we should note carefully the approximate and hesitant language that Ezekiel uses to describe the appearance of the Lord. Above the firmament there is the "likeness" of a throne. Seated on the throne is "a likeness as it were of a human form" (1:26). Upward from what seems the "appearance of his loins" is "gleaming bronze, like the appearance of fire enclosed round about" (1:27). There is a "brightness round about him" like the appearance of a rainbow (1:28). And then finally, "Such was the appearance of the likeness of the glory of the LORD" (1:28). He had something like that appearance, but the prophet will go no further than that. It is all careful, approximate language.

Forming the Sermon

There are statements in the Old Testament to the effect that some of the Israelites "saw the God of Israel." Exodus records that of Moses and Aaron and the elders who ate and drank with God on Mt. Sinai in what might be considered to have been the first "Lord's Supper" (Exod 24:10). Isaiah says it in the account of his vision (Isa 6:1). And we, in our naivete and ignorance of the overwhelming nature of God, would immediately ask, "What did God look like?" But the appearance of God is never described in the Old Testament, just as the appearance of Jesus Christ is never described in the New.

God hides his being, according to the Scriptures (cf. Isa 45:15), and we know him only from his deeds and words. Even in those passages that say some saw God, the gaze immediately shifts to describe only God's surroundings—"a pavement of sapphire stone" in Exodus (24:10), or the seraphim and the thresholds shaking and the smoke filling the heavenly temple in Isaiah (6:2–4). Moses beholds the form of the Lord, according to Numbers (12:8), and sees God's back as God passes by (Exod 33:23), but no further descriptions are given. As Exodus states, no one can see God and live (Exod 33:20).

Even in the account of creation, when we are told that we all are made in the image of God, God hides himself among his heavenly beings so that we cannot connect ourselves directly with his Person. "Let *us* make man in *our* image," God says to his heavenly court in Gen 1:26. So we all, male and female, are created in the image of the *'elohim*, the heavenly beings, including God (Gen 1:27; cf. Ps 8:5). We are *something* like God, but we are not God; we are creatures and God is our Creator (cf. Ps 100:3).

That is what Ezekiel is also saying in his account of his vision and call. The glory of the Lord, enthroned above the firmament, has something like the appearance as it were of a human form (Ezek 1:26), but not exactly. And human difference from God is then emphasized when the Lord addresses Ezekiel as "son of man," emphasizing the prophet's human weakness and mortality (Ezek 2:1, 3, 6, etc.). We cannot and we must not equate ourselves with the Creator who has made us.

Yet, God has something like the appearance of a human form, and this sort of description runs throughout the Old Testament. God is said to have hands and arms, legs and feet, eyes and a mouth.[2] We call those all anthropomorphisms— imaginative constructions of God in human form—and we do not take them literally. But the Old Testament insists on such descriptions, and perhaps it would be good for us to ask, Why?

First, the Old Testament, by using such descriptions, is insisting on the concrete locality of God. Someone once wisely remarked that God, in order to be everywhere, has first to be somewhere. God could distance himself from his sinful people (cf. Ezek 10–11). He was not to be identified with some generalized world soul or some ineffectual spiritual essence that human beings could discover any place and any time—an identification held by many in Israel's day and in our own. In fact, Deuteronomy stipulated that God was to be worshiped only at the place where he put his name, namely, in Jerusalem (Deut 12 passim). God was concrete, particularized, a specific Judge and Savior, who chose where he was to be found. That specificity was emphasized by the description of his form.

Second, by describing God as it does, the Old Testament continually insists on the personal nature of God. He was not

149

to be identified with the impersonal forces or objects of nature, and he was not to be imagined as an impersonal Primal Matrix from which all life has sprung, a great depth of amorphous Being from which we have come and to which we will return—this is also a falsehood of our time. No. God is supremely Person. In our Christian faith, he is One God in three concrete Persons, and so he meets us Person to person and demands from us the commitment of our total personhood: "You shall love the LORD your God with all your heart and with all your soul and with all your might" (Deut 6:4; Mark 12:30 and parallels)—Person to person and Heart to heart. You see, a great soul of nature or an impersonal Primal Matrix does not demand anything from us. This view of the divine makes ethics inconsequential, as we can see so clearly in our society. But God the particular Judge and Lord, King and Savior demands our total loyalty (Exod 20:3), on which all biblical faith and ethics are based.

This particularity, this concrete nature of God, this insistence on his personal nature finds its final revelation in the New Testament, then, in the most physical of anthropomorphisms, namely, in Jesus Christ, who is the incarnation of God in his Son. We now know who God is and can describe his words and deeds by telling the story of the life, death, and resurrection of our Lord Jesus Christ. Like Ezekiel, we cannot fully describe the actual appearance of God. But we know who he is and what he does and what he desires of us, and if we trust and obey him, that is all that we need for our salvation.

Notes

1. I consider chs. 40–48 of Ezekiel to be later additions to his book.

2. It should be noted, however, that God never has any sexuality in the Scriptures. He is neither male nor female, but rather the Holy One, utterly different from human beings. Gender differentiations are structures of creation (Gen 1:28), and cannot be applied to the Creator.

❧ 27 ❧

"The Saints
of the Most High"

DANIEL 7:1–3, 15–18

*T*HIS IS THE STATED OLD TESTAMENT LESSON FOR ALL
Saints' Day in Cycle C of the three-year lectionary. While
it prescribes that only eight verses be read from Dan 7, it is
necessary to understand the nature of the Book of Daniel and
the content of the whole of ch. 7 in order to grasp the
meaning of the passage.

Plumbing the Text

The Book of Daniel is an apocalypse, the only full-length
example of that type of literature that we have in the Old
Testament. Apocalypses deal with the end of human history,
with God's final judgment, and with the nature of the coming
new age of the Kingdom of God. Couched in often fantastic
and bizarre language to hide their message from the govern-
ing authorities, apocalypses and particularly Daniel are not
intended to predict the events that will take place in the
future history of our time or any contemporary time. Rather,
like Daniel, they are intended to encourage the faithful in a
time of persecution by showing them the glory in the new age
that awaits them beyond history, if they will only be faithful
to the end.

It is now acknowledged by all except fundamentalist scholars that the Book of Daniel was given its final form sometime between 167 and 164 B.C. It was intended to strengthen faithful Jews who were undergoing persecution by the Hellenistic ruler, Antiochus IV Epiphanes, who had desecrated the temple by offering a pig on its altar in 167 B.C. The first six chapters of Daniel therefore recount stories of faithful courage and obedience to God to inspire the readers to persevere in the same manner under Hellenistic persecution. Chapters 8–12 are visions of the overthrow and judgment of the tyrants, and of the glory that awaits the faithful. Our particular ch. 7 forms the heart of the book.

The four beasts that come up out of the sea (7:3–8) represent the Babylonian, Median, Persian, and Hellenistic empires, in that order. The eleventh little horn that grows up from the fourth beast is intended to stand for Antiochus IV Epiphanes.

Verses 9–14 portray the Day of Judgment at the end of history, when the beasts are judged by God, "the Ancient of Days," who appears in his fiery chariot (cf. Ezek 1:15–28). He opens the heavenly books and decrees the death of the eleventh little horn, while the rest of the beasts are stripped of their rule and held in captivity. Then comes "one like a son of man," to whom is given everlasting "dominion and glory" and the rule over all "peoples, nations, and languages" in a kingdom that will not pass away.

Finally, in vv. 15–28, an angel interprets the vision for Daniel, and from vv. 15–18 we learn that the "one like a son of man" is a corporate figure representing "the saints of the Most High" (vv. 18, 22, 27), that is, the authors and faithful Jews who persevere under persecution to the end. In a short time, dominion will be taken away from the hands of the tyrant and given to the saints in the faith, who will rule forever (v. 25).

In the apocalyptic books of 1 Enoch and the 2 Esdras in the Septuagint, the "Son of Man" is a preexistent heavenly figure, who will be the agent of judgment and salvation in the new age. But in our text, the words signify those human beings who are faithful to God.

In the New Testament Jesus uses the title "Son of Man" to refer exclusively to himself, perhaps to obscure his identity as the Messiah. He connects "Son of Man" with his present activity on earth (Mark 2:12 and parallels; Matt 8:20; 11:19), with his passion and resurrection (Mark 8:31 and parallels; 9:9, 11 and parallels; 10:33 and parallels), and with his future activity as Judge and Savior when he comes again at the end of time (Mark 8:38; 13:26 and parallels; 14:62 and parallels). Thus there is ample evidence to believe that Jesus was drawing on later Jewish apocalypticism, such as that found in 1 Enoch and 2 Esdras, to state his identity, although that has never been agreed upon by all scholars. Some think he used the title simply to identify himself as a human being (cf. the use of the term in Ezekiel). Others believe that Jesus was referring to a transcendent figure other than himself. Still others think Jesus never used the title at all and that it was added by the post-Easter community.[1]

It is clear in our passage, however, that "son of man" refers not to Jesus, but to faithful Jews. But because Jesus replaces Israel as the faithful Son of God, according to the New Testament (cf. Matt 2:14; John 15:1), the transfer of even Daniel's usage to Jesus would be appropriate. Nevertheless, in preaching from this stated text, it is probably best to refer "son of man" to the Jewish "saints of the Most High," as in Dan 7:18. Certainly that is the intention of the lectionary when the text is paired with Eph 1:11–23 and Luke 6:20–31.

Forming the Sermon

Are there no rewards for the faithful in heaven? Those who understand Christian doctrine know that we are justified by faith alone through the grace of God and that we do not work our way into eternal life by our good deeds. Anyone who tries to live a Christian life also knows, however, that faithfulness to God brings with it immeasurable treasures—peace with God that the world can neither give nor take away; joy in the community of God's people present, past, and future (the communion of saints); strength to do good in a world full of evil; and certain hope of everlasting life with the Father. We are granted grace in overflowing measure.

It is also the case in the New Testament that Jesus promises those who in truth follow him that their reward will be great in heaven.

> Blessed are you when men hate you, and when they exclude you and revile you, and cast out your name as evil, on account of the Son of man! Rejoice in that day, and leap for joy, for behold, your reward is great in heaven; for so their fathers did to the prophets. (Luke 6:22–23)

This promise is taken even further in Matthew:

> . . . in the new world, when the Son of man shall sit on his glorious throne, you who have followed me will also sit on twelve thrones, judging the twelve tribes of Israel. (Matt 19:28)

However we would interpret that quotation, many of the New Testament writers agree that the future eternal life of the faithful will be glorious. We will be glorified with Christ, writes Paul (Rom 8:17), and will share in the inheritance of the saints in light (1 Cor 1:12). We shall live and reign with Christ (2 Tim 2:11–12). We are destined for a glorious inheritance of the saints (Eph 1:18), and we will have a place among those who are sanctified by faith in Christ (Acts 26:18).

These verses all remind me of a homely example that I saw one time in a cartoon of Dennis the Menace. Looking up at the sky, Dennis exclaimed to his playmate, "If it's that beautiful on the bottom, imagine what it must be like on top!"

Apparently one adjective, more than others, characterizes the eternal life enjoyed by the faithful after earthly death: glorious. One has the feeling that the biblical writers simply strain at the boundaries of language to describe what is coming.

But according to Daniel and the New Testament, these things we know: we will be with Christ, who will be the same merciful, loving risen Lord that we have known from the

Scriptures; our life in the Kingdom of God will be eternal; and the glory of that life is past all of our imagining.

The Book of Daniel was written to assure suffering worshipers in their time of trial. While most of us are not persecuted for our faith—although many throughout our world are—we all know what it is to suffer. At times, we are tempted to give up our reliance on our Lord. Sometimes we think he hasn't heard one prayer we have uttered. Often we envy the prosperity and health of those who do not give a whit for God (cf. Ps 73). But Daniel tells us to persevere. Cling fast to your Lord. Pray to him continually. Trust his goodness and watchfulness over you. Study his Word. Never be ashamed of the gospel. For at the end, God will say to us, "Well done, good and faithful servant; you have been faithful over a little, I will set you over much; enter into the joy of your master" (Matt 25:21, 23 and parallels).

Notes

1. I am indebted to Reginald Fuller's article, "Son of man," for this material. *Harper's Bible Dictionary* (ed. P. J. Achtemeier; San Francisco: Harper & Row, 1985), 981.

28

Marry a Harlot

HOSEA 1:2–9

THIS PASSAGE IS THE STATED OLD TESTAMENT LESSON for the seventeenth Sunday after Pentecost or in Ordinary Time in cycle C of the three year lectionary. The lectionary joins these verses with v. 10, but vv. 1 through 9 form a complete unit in themselves and should be treated separately.

There are so many commentaries on the Book of Hosea[1] that it scarcely seems necessary to deal with this text as a "hard" passage. Yet the history of the interpretation of the passage reveals how "hard" these verses have been for some commentators to accept, and still today, many pious readers are offended by them.

Plumbing the Text

Hosea's ministry took place during the last years of the reign of Jeroboam II (786–746 B.C.) in northern Israel. That kingdom was enjoying a stable government and economic prosperity, but there was a great disparity between the rich and the poor, the law courts were corrupt, cultic practices were shot through with the syncretistic worship of the fertility gods of Baal, and public morality and covenant responsibility were lost to the populace.

In such a society, Hosea is commanded to marry a "woman of harlotry" *('eshet zenunim)* and to have "children of harlotry."

Gomer's harlotry probably consists in the fact that she has engaged in sexual relations with priests and laity in the cult of Baal, perhaps once, perhaps sporadically or continually. It was believed that by such cultic practice, Baal would be coerced by sympathetic magic to make the woman fertile and able to bear children. Gomer is not a prostitute in our sense of the term, wandering the streets for customers, although perhaps later she falls into such degradation (cf. 3:1–3).

Attempts have been made to soften the words of Hosea 1:2–9. Some commentators have maintained that Gomer was a virgin and a faithful wife when the prophet first married her, but that she then became adulterous. To substantiate their argument they point out that Hosea is said to be the father of only the first child, Jezreel.

If such were the case, however, the reason and meaning for God's command would be destroyed. In the Book of Hosea, God is "married" to Israel, who is his beloved wife by covenant. But Israel is an adulterous wife. She has run after other lovers, namely after the Baal fertility gods from whom she expects to have life and fertility, both in nature and in human relationships. Hosea's marriage to Gomer, the harlot, is the shocking sign and symbol of the fact that God's bride Israel is also a harlot. Any faithfulness that Israel had is long in the past, and God is dealing with the present. Marry a harlot now, he commands Hosea, because Israel is a harlot now.

The three children born to Gomer symbolize God's reaction to Israel's harlotry, and indeed, their symbolic names begin God's action of judgment toward his adulterous people.

The first born son is named Jezreel, not because God has changed his mind about the prophetic revolution that was commanded by the Lord and that toppled the Omri dynasty and put Jehu on the throne at Jezreel (2 Kgs 9:1–13; 10:10). Rather, the son Jezreel symbolizes the fact that Jehu's dynasty, which first opposed the worship of Baal (2 Kgs 10:18–28), nevertheless continued the worship of the golden calves that Jeroboam I had erected at Bethel and at Dan (2 Kgs 10:29–31).

The fact that the next two children are not specifically said to have Hosea as their father is probably because the style becomes increasingly succinct in vv. 6 and 8 and the word "to him" *(lo)* is simply omitted for stylistic reasons. This does not present evidence that Gomer was a virgin at her wedding.

The daughter, "Not pitied" *(lo -ruhamah)*, sets forth the ominous fact that the Lord will no longer be moved to respond in mercy and tender mother-love to the need of his people. But the name of the second son, "Not my people" *(lo - ammi)* is the climactic judging symbol in the passage. God now declares that the covenant is broken; he is no longer Israel's God, and they are no longer his people. "I will be your God, and you shall be my people," was the standard covenant formula, found throughout the Old Testament (Exod 6:7; Lev 26:12; Jer 7:23; 11:4, et al.). Such a formula no longer applies. God has divorced his wife Israel, because she has been unfaithful to him. And Hosea's marriage to a harlot is the sign of that broken relationship.

We should notice Hosea's immediate obedience to God's command. God says "Go, take . . . ," and the text testifies, "So he went and took . . . "

Forming the Sermon

God commands his prophet to marry a woman of harlotry. Would God issue such a command, and would a prophet of God obey it? Imagine what Hosea's father, Beeri, would say about such a marriage. And imagine the gossip that circulated among the neighbors. Why on earth would a man of God, a prophet of the Lord, marry such a wanton woman? She's been down there at the shrine of Baal, taking into her bed every no-good that pays his money to the priests. Hosea must be out of his mind.

But I cannot help wondering why anyone in our society is shocked. After all, we are accustomed to harlotrous and adulterous relationships. For example, in the movie "Pretty Woman" the leading man does in fact marry a prostitute. We are used to harlotry, aren't we, and the pollsters tell us that 20 percent of all marriages in this country are marked by adultery. The thing that amazes us about that statistic is not the 20 percent adultery figure; it's the 80 percent of faithfulness. We thought adultery was much more widespread than that!

Certainly sexual promiscuity is rampant. The military has been having a terrible time controlling the relationship between the sexes. And the majority of people in this country think there is nothing wrong with pre-marital sex. Certainly every young person on every college campus has to come to terms with it. And the question on every date is, Should this lead to bed, and if so, how soon? As for TV, we all know that every romantic encounter portrayed is presupposed to include fornication, and that seldom is any promiscuous relation portrayed as having any consequences. So what's the big deal? What's so terrible about the Lord commanding his prophet to marry a harlot?

The aspect of the text that bothers us is that God commands such a marriage. And that does not fit our conception of God. After all, the Lord is the deity who commands, "You shall not commit adultery" and "you shall not covet your neighbor's wife" (Exod 20:14, 17). Jesus is the one who taught that out of the heart come "evil thoughts, fornication, theft, murder, adultery" (Mark 7:21 and parallels). And his apostle Paul writes that persons committing such offenses will not inherit the Kingdom of God (1 Cor 6:9–11). So you see, we still have a little hint of the image of God in ourselves. While we may be a promiscuous and adulterous generation, we do not want a God who commands his prophet to take part in our loose affairs. We may be evil, but we want our God to be wholly good, because his goodness may be the only thing that finally saves us from our evil. Deep down inside of our wanton hearts, do we not sense that truth?

God is totally good—and loving and merciful. And his goodness and mercy are the only things that can save our wandering souls. And in order to save us, all through the Scriptures, God asks his servants to suffer for the sake of our

159

salvation. He tells Hosea, in order to burn my Word into the eyes and hearts of a harlot Israel, go, take to yourself a wife of harlotry, and then weep, Hosea, weep over those children playing in your courtyard who are the doomed products of that harlotry.

And Jesus, my Son, my beloved Son, go, take upon yourself all the sins of this world in the shape of a cross, and weep, Jesus, weep over Jerusalem and this whoring world, so that perhaps finally it may learn that in love and faithfulness to me alone lie its redemption and hope for the future.

God gathers up and incarnates our sins before our eyes—in the person of his prophet Hosea and finally and fully in our dying Savior upon a cross. And those incarnations are intended to lead us to repentance—repentance for all of our promiscuity, all of our fornication and adultery, all of our faithless disobedience of God's clear Word.

Goodness knows, our sexual sins do not form the majority of our trespasses. Our pride, our selfishness, our killing, and our greed still rank at the top of the list. But our faithless sexuality has taken an awful toll in our time—in broken families, in disturbed children, in rampant abortion, and in venereal disease—and this passage from Hosea speaks to that faithlessness too toward our God. Surely our response to our shock at this passage should be repentance and renewed commitment to our God of goodness.

Notes

1. E.g., my commentary, *Minor Prophets I.*

❧ 29 ❧

God's Use of
Natural Catastrophes

AMOS 4:4–13

WHEN STUDYING THIS PASSAGE IN A SEMINARY CLASS-
room, I have often asked my students if they believe
what it says. Invariably the answer has been "no." We twen-
tieth-century moderns do not think that God uses the natural
world in this fashion. So this passage presents difficulties
for us.

There are many other passages in the Old Testament
that give the same testimony about God's use of the natural
world, but this one brings the question of whether this really
happens sharply into focus, and so we can concentrate on it.
What we say about this Amos text may then be applied to
other similar testimonies.

Plumbing the Text

Amos 4:4–13 is a unit, and it concerns Israel's communion with God. The people of the northern kingdom in the
eighth century B.C. believe that by lavish worship practices at
their shrines of Bethel and Gilgal, they can guarantee their
relationship with the Lord. All of the sacrifices and cultic
practices mentioned can be understood as communion meals
or peace offerings to God. Bethel, located just south of the

capital of Samaria, was the site of the king's northern sanctuary (Amos 7:13); Gilgal was a popular place of pilgrimage, near
Jericho.

Far from accepting their worship of him, God declares in
this judgment oracle that such worship is "rebellion" against
his rule—a political term signifying subversion. The northern
kingdom abounds in unjust social practices and syncretistic
worship, and therefore the Israelites' supposed communion
with their Lord is false to the core.

God declares in this text that he has repeatedly tried to
warn and discipline his errant folk, subjecting them to famine
(vv. 6–9), disease (v. 10) and military defeat (v. 10), in the
attempt to make them understand that he is in charge of their
life. All of the disasters that God has brought upon Israel
constitute some of the curses that Lev 26 and Deut 28 say
will fall upon those who fail to keep the covenant with the
Lord. Israel knew the covenant stipulations, and she should
have been warned and repented when a covenant curse fell
upon her. But she did not take warning. "Yet you did not
return to me," God repeats five times.

Therefore, God will return to Israel. He will enter into
the relationship that the Israelites so desire (v. 12), but it will
be a relationship of judgment. Israel will meet her God, and
she will be destroyed.

Verse 13 then describes the awesome character of the
God who comes to meet his people. He formed the mountains
like a potter working with clay. He gives all creatures their
breath of life. (The proper reading here is "breath" or "spirit"
or "breath of life," not "wind."[1]) He reveals to human beings
his plan for the world. He can turn the morning light into
darkness and tread down all the idolatrous high places of
worship. He is the Lord God Sebaoth, ruler of all the hosts of
heaven and of earth.

Forming the Sermon

We may believe that God works in human history, influ-
encing the desires and directions of human hearts, but in our

modern scientific age we have a very difficult time believing
that he works in the processes of nature. The natural world
is largely a closed system for us. We believe that God created
the world in the first place, setting it up with its own natural
laws. But now many persons think that the realm of nature
works automatically, according to those inherent laws. God
does not interfere, at least not very often, in the operation of
natural laws. Occasionally God may answer a prayer for healing; occasionally he may save someone from natural disaster.
We call those "miracles." But for the most part, the natural
world proceeds in its accustomed round, according to the
built-in laws that our scientists may then study and describe.

In short, we have almost totally secularized the world of
nature. That is, we describe it as a realm from which God is
absent. We give lip-service to the belief that God is the Lord,
not only of history but also of the natural realm. But in our
day-by-day view of our environment, God does not interfere
with nature's automatic processes.

This passage from Amos directly contradicts that view,
of course. It maintains that the Lord has given or withheld
rain, that he has sent blight and mildew and locusts to ruin
crops, that he has infested the populace with disease, as well
as caused military defeats—all in the effort to warn his people
to return to true worship and obedience of him.

We do not like that view of God. Probably we think it is
a harsh way to get anyone to repent. And we certainly do not
believe that famine or drought or disease are the results of God's
actions. They have occurred naturally, and should be dealt
with as such. We are not about to return to a pre-scientific
view of the world in which illness and natural disaster are
God's punishments or even warnings about sinfulness.

The whole of the Bible states otherwise, contradicting
our closed understanding. In Gen 8:22, for example, God
promises that the cycle of the seasons and day and night will
continue, not because nature works automatically, but because God has promised that such cycles will continue—and
he always keeps his promises. In his Sermon on the Mount,
Jesus teaches that God feeds the birds of the air and clothes

163

the lilies of the field in a glory exceeding that of Solomon (Matt 6:26, 28–30), and later he assures his disciples that not a sparrow "falls to the ground without your Father's will" (Matt 10:29).

Indeed, the Bible is full of the testimony that God controls the appearance and movement of heavenly bodies (e.g., Job 38:31–33), and that he can use the stars and sun for his own purposes (e.g., Job 9:7). Thus, at the crucifixion of our Lord the sun's light fails and there is darkness over the whole land from the sixth hour to the ninth (Luke 23:44–45).

Similarly, God is in charge of earth's geology. He can form the mountains or remove them (e.g., Job 9:5); he can cause the land to heave up and then sink (e.g., Amos 8:8; 9:5). At the moment of Christ's death on the cross, therefore, the earth shakes, the rocks are split, and tombs are opened (Matt 27:51–52).

Throughout the Scriptures, God also controls meteorology; God determines whether there will be wind or snow, hail or dew and hoarfrost (e.g., Ps 147:15–18). He gives food to all creatures (Ps 104:20–21) and sustains all alive with his breath of life (Ps 104:29–30). In short, all the processes of nature are dependent on God's faithfulness in maintaining their order. And when God wills, he can use the natural world for blessing his people or for judging them.[2] God is indeed, in the world-view of the Scripture, the Lord of heaven and earth, with all their processes and manifestations.

What are to make of that? Can we combine such biblical testimony with a modern scientific world-view? More specifically, can we accept as true what Amos says here in ch. 4? I believe we can.

First, let us accept as true what the Bible says about God's relation to the natural world. He is in fact the Lord of nature, and the natural world is sustained in its orderly working by his faithfulness. G. K. Chesterton once poetically suggested that God says to the sun every morning, "do it again."[3] God, in his common grace, shed upon us all, prevents our cosmos from returning to chaos, and preserves for us the wonders of the natural world. In Jesus' words, "He makes his sun rise on the evil and on the good, and sends rain on the just and on the unjust" (Matt 5:45). Or in the words of Ezra's prayer,

> Thou art the LORD, thou alone; thou hast made heaven, the heaven of heavens, with all their host, the earth and all that is on it, the seas and all that is in them; and thou preservest all of them. (Neh 9:6)

Thus, when our scientists study the orderly processes of the natural world, what they are doing, whether they acknowledge it or not, is describing the orders that God is sustaining in his faithfulness.

Does that mean, however, that God is punishing us when some natural disaster or illness devastates our lives? Should we see all calamities as God's work? When a monsoon drowns helpless peasants, is that God's punishment of them? When children die in a drought and famine, is that God's desire? If a nursing home's roof collapses on its aged residents in an earthquake, is that God's wrathful judgment? Of course not.

The second thing we must realize is that human stupidity and sin often bring such calamities upon human beings. A corrupt government that will not feed its populace and that hoards a nation's resources for itself can lead and has led to the starvation of millions of children. Homes built on flood plains are sooner or later going to be washed away. If nuclear plants, cities, and nursing homes are erected on earthquake faults, they run the daily risk of being destroyed. God has indeed set up orderly processes in our world, and we need to heed that order and take warning from the insights and knowledge of our scientists and scholars. We bring a lot of so-called "natural disasters" upon ourselves by our indifference, our selfishness, our greed, our sin. And God certainly desires none of those.

But God sometimes uses natural disasters and illnesses to warn us and to try to get us to turn around and mend our sinful ways, as our text in Amos 4 says. To be sure, there are Scripture texts that mention natural disaster that God has not used at all (e.g., Gen 12:10). God is, nevertheless, the Lord of nature, and he can use it for his purposes.

The third thing that must be noted is that we should not point to every calamity as God's judgment on sin. Jesus makes that clear in John 9:3. Our attitude toward others' suffering must not be self-righteous and accusatory, but merciful and helping. But when a disaster falls on us, certainly every Christian should ask, "Is God trying to tell me something?" Every illness and every calamity should lead us to examine our lives and to ask ourselves if we have indeed been faithful to our covenant with God. That is the question the Israelites in our Amos text never asked themselves. They never turned. They never repented. And so disaster came upon them. God does in fact discipline us, as a good father disciplines his children (cf. Deut 8:5). God constantly tries to guide us, by all sorts of means, because he wants us to live abundantly. Always we should be alert and open to his loving guidance, for we cannot have abundant life apart from him.

Notes

1. The word *ruakh* can have any of these meanings depending on the context.

2. For a full discussion of the dependence of the natural world on God, see my book, *Nature, God, and Pulpit,* ch. 5.

3. "The Ethics of Elfland," in *Orthodoxy* (1908; repr., New York: Doubleday, 1900), ch. 4.

❦ 30 ❧

"The LORD Repented"

AMOS 7:1–6

IN DEALING WITH THIS TEXT, WE WILL BE ONLY SECONDAR-ily interested in the contents of Amos' visions and their place in his prophecies, since those have been amply explicated in numerous commentaries.[1] For purposes of this volume, we want to concentrate on the twofold statement in vv. 3 and 6 that "the LORD repented." That has troubled many readers of the Bible. How can it be that the Lord repents?

Plumbing the Text

These two visions form the first two units in a series of four visions (7:1–3, 4–6, 7–9; 8:1–3) that were given to Amos at various times while he was in a state of prophetic ecstasy, a state through which God often communicated with his prophets in Israel. The series is interrupted by the encounter with the high priest Amaziah at the king's sanctuary at Bethel (7:10–17).

The first two visions announce the nature of the future judgments that God intends to bring on Israel for her pride, injustice, and phony worship.

The vision recounted in vv. 1–3 reveals to Amos that God is forming a locust hoard to descend upon Israel in the late spring, after the second planting upon which Israel is dependent for food during the dry summer months. Because locust plagues could destroy every shred of vegetation, and even the bark on trees, such a judgment would threaten Israel with extinction.

The second vision, detailed in vv. 4–6, which the prophet probably received in midsummer, shows the Lord preparing a judgment of supernatural fire that will burn up that land and even "the great deep," that is, the waters under the earth.

When Amos sees these awful judgments that God is preparing to inflict upon his sinful people, the prophet intercedes for his people in prayer to God. In v. 2, Amos asks that the Lord forgive Jacob's (Israel's) sin out of pity for the weakness and smallness of the people. In v. 5, because forgiveness was not granted, the prophet's petition simply asks God to cease, to stop preparing the judgment, again appealing to the pitiful nature of the people. In both instances, the text says that "the LORD repented" and abolished the prepared judgment. "The LORD repented." That is our subject.

Forming the Sermon

When we speak of repentance, we ordinarily think in terms of repenting from sin, of turning around (*sabeb* in the Hebrew), and guiding our lives in the opposite direction. Obviously that is not the meaning of God's repentance. God does not sin. Our Father in heaven is perfect (Matt 5:48), and his Son Jesus Christ is without sin (Heb 4:15). Thus, a different verb *(nihem)* is used of God's repentance.

God is said to repent numerous times in the Old Testament, and several different meanings are given to the word. In Gen 6:6, the Bible states that "the LORD was sorry that he had made man on the earth," and the verb for "repented" is used, just as in 1 Sam 15:11, 34, the Lord repents that he has made Saul king over Israel. So when God repents, it can mean that he regrets a former action of his that has subsequently produced ill results. God has made human beings, and they have turned out to be evil. He appointed Saul king, and Saul disobeyed. God regrets these former actions of his, because human beings have corrupted God's intended result. And that grieves God to his heart (Gen 6:6).

However, in Old Testament passages, including Amos 7:1–6, God's repentance is his decision not to send judgment upon an individual or upon the nation. In short, God changes his mind. He decides not to punish for sin. The verb for "repent" can have the meaning of "to have compassion" or "to pity," and that is involved here in our Amos text. The prophet points out to God how pitiful and weak the supposedly prosperous, bustling, strong Israel really is, and God in compassion for his pitiful people takes back his judgment upon them.

Frequently God undergoes such change and decides not to punish (Exod 32:14; 2 Sam 24:16; Jonah 3:10; Jer 26:19). In fact, so frequent is such repentance on the part of God, that this characteristic of his nature is included in one of Israel's oldest, central creeds. The Lord God is "gracious and merciful, slow to anger, and abounding in steadfast love, and repents of evil," says the creed (Joel 2:13; Jonah 3:9). Throughout the Old Testament, God is above all a God of love and compassion.

The fact that God changes his mind gives us pause, however. We are used to thinking in Greek terms, in which God is the unmoved Mover, without a shadow of turning, whose will and actions are fixed and certain. Indeed, there is one passage in the Old Testament that sets forth that fixity of God's nature:

> God is not man, that he should lie,
>   or a son of man, that he should repent.
> Has he said, and will he not do it?
>   Or has he spoken, and will he not fulfil it?
>   (Num 23:19=1 Sam 15:29)

It is rather unsettling to think otherwise, to believe that God can change his mind.

The important fact to note in our text, however, is that the Lord changes his mind in response to Amos' intercessory prayer. And that is repeatedly true in several of the passages where God's repentance is mentioned. In Exod 32:14, the Lord decides not to wipe out Israel for its worship of the golden calf, because Moses intercedes in prayer for the people. It is David's intercession in 2 Sam 24:16 that turns aside God's threat to destroy Jerusalem.

Similarly, several texts state that the people's repentance and entreaty and renewed trust may cause God to "repent" of the judgment he has intended upon them (Jonah 3:9–10; Joel 2:14; Jer 18:8; 26:3, 13, 19; 42:10), whereas in another text Israel's inability to repent of its sin means that God will not repent of his judgment upon them (Ezek 24:14).

There are two implications for us. First of all, we see a clear indication in this Amos text and those similar to it that intercessory prayer may be effective. Amos' prayer leads God to change his mind about what he is going to do.

In fact, intercession for their sinful people is one of the functions of an Old Testament prophet. Moses, the first and greatest of the prophets, several times intercedes with God for his sinful people and turns aside God's judgment on them (Exod 32:11–14; 34:9; Deut 9:13–29; 10:10–11). Jeremiah intercedes so often for Judah that God has finally to tell him to be silent (7:16; 11:14; cf. 15:1). A prophetic voice in Third Isaiah says that he will never keep silent until the Lord brings salvation to Jerusalem (Isa 62:1). And Ezekiel proclaims that a prophet is false if he will not intercede for Judah when she is being attacked by God for her sin (Ezek 13:5).

It is the duty of the men and women of God to utter intercessory prayers for their sinful society in order to turn aside God's judgments on it. And of course that is the prophetic function that our Lord fulfilled on the cross. Despite our sin that crucified him, he prayed for us, "Father, forgive them for they know not what they do" (Luke 23:34). Indeed, the apostle Paul tells us that the risen Christ continues to intercede for us at the right hand of the Father (Rom 8:34). And when "we do not know how to pray as we ought, the Spirit intercedes for us with sighs too deep for words" (Rom 8:26–27).

The implication therefore is that we should not doubt the efficacy of intercessory prayer. As Jesus taught, we "ought always to pray and not to lose heart" (Luke 18:1). We should "pray at all times in the Spirit" (Eph 6:18), "pray constantly" (1 Thess 5:17), and "pray for one another" (Jas 5:16).

Intercessory prayer does not bind God to a course of action, of course. God is always free, as the prophet Joel (2:14) and even the alien king of Nineveh knew (Jonah 3:9). Because God is good and wishes only good for us, we can trust that he answers prayer according to our genuine best interests. Nevertheless, intercessory prayer may lead to a change in God's actions toward us. The whole of Scripture testifies to that fact.

The second noteworthy fact we can glean from Amos 7:1–6 and others is that our future is not fixed in the purpose and plan of God. There is no determinism in the Scriptures. Rather, human history can be characterized as a vast dialogue between God and human beings. God says and does something. Human beings react to that in faithfulness or disobedience, and God in turn reacts accordingly. He may swiftly punish wrongdoing. He may gather up evil and use it for his purpose, as he did with the cross. He may let the evil continue for a time and loose us from his hand, simply letting us reap the consequences of our own wrong-doing (Rom 1:24–31). He may suspend his judgment if repentance and reformation are forthcoming, as in Ezek 18.

There are a multitude of ways in which God may work with us. But throughout the Scriptures, God takes human decisions and actions seriously, and he is constantly adjusting, redirecting, sometimes rearranging our lives and our history accordingly so as to further his loving purpose for the world.

Scripture tells us that one factor in human history remains constant, however, and that is God's goal. God is working to bring his kingdom on earth even as it is in heaven. We know that the kingdom will come, no matter what we sinful human beings believe or do, because the kingdom has begun to come in Jesus Christ (Mark 1:15; Luke 11:20; 17:21; Matt 3:2), and because all the forces of sin and of death have been unable to defeat him. Christians know what the end of human history will be, and they know who will be there at the end. Every knee will bow and every tongue confess that Jesus

Christ is Lord, to the glory of God the Father (Phil 2:11). All things will be united in Christ (Eph 1:10), and God will be all in all. In the meantime, God takes very seriously our decisions along the way toward that final salvation.

To be sure, none of us will ever deserve an entrance into the eternal life of the kingdom. But in faith, we can trust that the righteousness of Christ will avail for us, and that God will save us because of our Lord. That decision to trust Jesus Christ every day is also a decision that God takes very seriously.

Notes

1. E.g., my commentary, *Minor Prophets I.*

❦ 31 ❦

"The Day of the Lord"

ZEPHANIAH 1:14–18

*F*EW PASSAGES IN THE OLD TESTAMENT HAVE BEEN MORE widely used in the liturgy of the church, in literature, and in sacred and secular music than has this hymn on the Day of the Lord. The Latin Vulgate reads the beginning of v. 15 as *Dies irae,* and it is under that title that the passage has been used in countless poems and musical numbers, as well as in the Latin Mass.

The church has also incorporated the passage into its lectionaries, coupling it with eschatological passages from 1 Thessalonians and from Matt 24 or 25. Thus, the Old Testament concept of the Day of the Lord has become connected in the Christian faith with the second coming of Christ, with the resurrection from the dead, and with the last judgment. Typical of our society, however, sermons on this passage are rarely heard today, because many believe that God never judges anybody.

Plumbing the Text

While Zeph 1:14–18 forms a separate poem, these verses should be read as a sequel to the preceding vv. 7–13. The whole of 1:7–18 then forms an announcement of the imminent coming of the Day of the Lord.

What is that Day? First, it is not to be understood as one particular day, but rather as a period of time in the indefinite future. Second, it will be that time when God will "rend the heavens and come down," to use the words of Isaiah (64:1), to exercise his final destroying judgment on all of his enemies, to exalt his faithful, and to set up his kingdom over all the earth. Contrary to the New Testament understanding, it will mark not the end of human history, but the transformation of human life and the world.

Such a concept of the Day of the Lord had ancient roots in Israel. It arose in Israel's theology of the "Holy War," in the time of the tribal federation and of the Judges, when Israel conducted its battles according to strict cultic rules (hence the name "Holy War"). During those early battles, the Old Testament testifies that God, the Divine Warrior, fought on behalf of his people with supernatural means (cf. Josh 2:9, 24; 5:1; 7:5; 10:11; Judg 5:4–5, etc.). The popular belief therefore arose in Israel that the Lord would always fight for her against her enemies.

Amos, in the eighth century B.C., was the first prophet to turn the popular belief upside down. God would destroy not only Israel's enemies, he preached, but also Israel herself for all of her unfaithfulness to her covenant with the Lord (cf. Amos 5:18–20). In this announcement of God's judgment on Israel, Amos was followed by Isaiah, Ezekiel, Joel, Malachi, and here, Zephaniah.

The Day of the Lord came to be understood, therefore, as an ominous time of God's anger and wrath against the wicked, as a day of darkness and gloom, as a day of trumpet blast and battle cry, with God the Divine Warrior summoning his heavenly hosts to do battle with him against his enemies (cf. Joel 3:14–17). That is the picture we find in Zeph 1:7–18.

In this passage in Zephaniah, God comes to judge the entire earth (v. 18), but Israel's sins are specifically mentioned. God's covenant people have engaged in idolatry and syncretism (1:5, 8–9). But even worse, they have become totally indifferent toward the Lord and think of him as unnecessary. Verse 12 gives the heart of the indictment. The people are "thickening upon their lees." The figure is taken from wine-making, in which wine had to be poured off of its sediment before it became thick and syrupy and ruined. Israel has been ruined. She has said in her heart—the locus of all commitment and love—that God will do neither good nor evil, that God will do nothing at all. In short, Israel's sin is the sin of pride. She thinks that God is unnecessary and that she can run her own life. God therefore comes on his Day to do his people to death, along with all sinners on earth.

Zephaniah does have a concept of a remnant, as can be seen in 3:9–13. Those who will be saved in the judgment are those who humbly put their trust in God as their sole refuge and Lord. Human pride and self-sufficiency are gone, and the faithful remnant dwells in the peaceable realm of God's kingdom, with God in their midst, rejoicing with them (3:14–17).

Forming the Sermon

Perhaps few biblical passages are more relevant to our time and society than is this text from Zephaniah. Two characteristics of our modern life make it so.

First, many in our time who do believe in God nevertheless do not think he judges anyone. God, in our popular imagination—as in Israel's—is a kindly figure who can be called upon when we are in distress, who often blesses our lives with good things, and who can always be counted on to forgive, no matter what we do. Thus, anything goes in our time; we have seen it all, and some have done it all. And God's attitude toward our actions and lives is one only of kindly love.

Second, our society is marked by a widespread secularism that believes, like Judah in Zephaniah's time, that God does nothing at all. God is a totally inactive and indifferent figure, if indeed he exists at all. The lives of human beings are entirely in their own hands, for better or for ill, although sometimes luck or chance plays a part. Ultimately, we choose our own paths and fashion our own destinies, and God has nothing to do with them.

175

In response to this latter characteristic of our age, Zephaniah and the whole of Scripture tell us that we have an ineradicable relation with God that is present at every moment of our daily lives. We are made in the image of God, declares Genesis, which means we stand always in relation to him. God knows even when we sit down and when we rise, proclaims the Psalmist (Ps 139:2). He numbers each hair on our heads, teaches Jesus (Matt 10:30). And always he is at work in our lives and in our world (John 5:17). We therefore are responsible to this God, whom we cannot escape, for all we say and do (cf. Matt 25:31–46; Mark 9:37 and parallels), and far from being a deity who can be ignored, he is a God to whom we must answer.

Zephaniah and the whole of Scripture also tell us that God is not mocked. Whatever persons sow, they will also reap, writes Paul (Gal 6:7). We are always accountable to God and his will, and there will in fact come that final Day when we stand before the judgment seat of God.

Further, in the New Testament, God's judgment of us on the Day of the Lord will be rendered in terms of our relationship to Jesus Christ. "Everyone who acknowledges me before men [and women]," Jesus teaches, "I also will acknowledge before my Father who is in heaven; but whoever denies me before men [and women], I will also deny before my Father who is in heaven" (Matt 10:32 and parallels). We all will stand before the judgment seat of Christ and be judged in terms of our love and obedience toward him (2 Cor 5:10; cf. Matt 25:31–46). So most of the parables of Jesus call us not only to decide who he is ("Who do you say that I am?" [Mark 12:20]) but also to examine our lives in terms of the commands that he has laid upon us. Jesus says, "Not every one who says to me, 'Lord, Lord,' shall enter the kingdom of heaven, but he who does the will of my Father who is in heaven" (Matt 7:21 and parallels).

"He will come again to judge the quick and the dead," we confess in the Apostles' Creed, and there will take place the choice between who will be chosen for eternal life and who will be rejected. Two men will be at work, Jesus teaches in Matt 24, and one will be taken into the kingdom, and one will be left outside. Two women will be preparing a meal, and one will be taken and one left. And so the admonition of Jesus in the gospels is to "Watch!" and be prepared, for we do not know when the Lord will come. It may be "in the evening, or at midnight, or at cockcrow [the hour of temptation], or in the morning" (Mark 13:35). Or perhaps Christ will return this afternoon!

Yes, Zephaniah's proclamation of the coming of the Day of the Lord is pertinent indeed to our generation that is "thickening upon its lees," and we need to be warned that the Day may be one of wrath and ruin, of distress and darkness, of devastation and gloom, as the prophet told a Judah whose sin was equal to ours.

But the second chapter in Zephaniah's book tells us how to escape calamity: "Repent!" Zephaniah calls for a feast of repentance in 2:1. "Seek the LORD . . . seek righteousness, seek humility; perhaps you may be hidden on the day of the wrath of the LORD" (2:3). God in his freedom has the ability to forgive us, if we turn to him with sincere hearts and deeds.

Indeed, is it not in the recognition of our sinfulness and in throwing ourselves totally on the mercy of God in Jesus Christ that we may be saved? None of us has been a profitable servant. None of us has been always useful in the purpose of the Lord. All of us appear before Christ in the filthy rags of fault rather than in the pure mantle of righteousness. And our only prayer can be, "God, be merciful to me, a sinner" (Luke 18:13)!

But that is the glory of the Christian gospel. That is the good news for all people. Through the death and resurrection of Jesus Christ—who comes to judge the quick and the dead—God shows that he is above all else a God of mercy and of forgiveness, whose love always overcomes his wrath, and whose desire that we live far surpasses his wish for our death. In Jesus Christ, we are forgiven, and in him, we may be judged righteous in the Day.

177

❧ 32 ❧

The Golden Lampstand

ZECHARIAH 4:1–14

"NOT BY MIGHT, NOR BY POWER, BUT BY MY SPIRIT, SAYS the LORD of hosts" (v. 6). Innumerable sermons have been preached on these words, and it formed a favorite text of preachers in the past two generations. However, the words were ripped frequently out of their context and made to apply to almost any situation. Now those preachers who realize that separate verses cannot so easily be separated from their setting hesitate to preach from this passage in Zechariah because of the difficult symbolism involved in it. Yet the passage bears a marvelous message for the church that should not be ignored from the pulpit.

Plumbing the Text

The ministry of the prophet Zechariah overlapped that of the prophet Haggai by almost two months, and the historical setting of both prophets was similar. They were among the second group of Babylonian exiles to return to Jerusalem, under the leadership of the Davidic Zerubbabel. Jerusalem still lay in ruins, and while the foundation of the temple had been laid earlier, the work had been discontinued because of Samaritan opposition and the meager resources and hardships of the populace. Haggai's prophecies are concerned with the temple rebuilding.

Zechariah's emphases are somewhat different, however. He tells us that on February 15, 519 B.C. he was granted a series of eight bizarre visions, as well as a number of prophetic oracles, which are now found in the first two sections of his book (1:7–2:13 and 3:1–6:15). Our passage forms the fifth of those visions.

In an ecstatic state, described as being wakened out of sleep to see reality (v. 1), Zechariah is shown a costly golden lampstand in the form of a cylindrical column. It is not a menorah or a lampstand like that in Solomon's temple (1 Kgs 7:49) but rather is tapered upward and topped with a bowl of oil. Around the rim of this main bowl are seven smaller bowls, each with seven wicks around its edges, making a total of forty-nine lights. On each side of the lampstand is an olive tree with its branch overshadowing the main bowl, so that it feeds oil directly through a golden pipe to the lampstand, apart from human processing.

Zechariah asks three times what this strange vision means (vv. 4, 11, 12), and after the angel speaks in vv. 6–7 and Zechariah himself delivers the oracle of vv. 8–10, he is finally given an explanation (v. 10b–14). The oil in the vision represents the Spirit of God. The forty-nine lights, which are also called "eyes" because the eye was understood as a source of light (cf. Matt 6:22), symbolize the covenant people of Israel who are to shine forth into all the world. The two olive trees on each side of the lampstand represent the "two anointed," the high priest and the Davidic king or Messiah. Thus they are the mediators of the "oil" that feeds the light of Israel, that is, they are mediators of the Spirit of God. Interrupting this vision, in vv. 7–10a, is the promise that Zerubbabel will put the topstone to the temple building, thus completing its construction.

The meaning of the vision therefore is contained in v. 6. Israel will be a light to the world only as she is supplied with the Spirit of God through the mediation of the high priest and Davidic king. Her own "might," which means all of her resources, and her own "power," which signifies all of her resolve, are insufficient. The light of God can shine forth through his people to the world only as they rely on God's Spirit.

Forming the Sermon

"You are the light of the world," Jesus told his disciples (Matt 5:14). The followers of Jesus Christ have inherited the task first given to Israel, to be a light shining in the darkness for all peoples everywhere.

It is significant that throughout the Scriptures God's abundant life that he wishes to give to humankind, God's salvation, is described in terms of "light." "The LORD is my light and my salvation; whom shall I fear?" (Ps 27:1). "The people who walked in darkness have seen a great light" (Isa 9:2). "In him was life, and the life was the light of men. The light shines in the darkness, and the darkness has not overcome it" (John 1:4). "You are . . . God's own people, that you may declare the wonderful deeds of him who called you out of darkness into his marvelous light" (1 Pet 2:9). Jesus Christ is "the true light that enlightens every man" (John 1:9), and to those who trust him, his truth is light (cf. Ps 43:3), his words give light (cf. Ps 119:130), and by his light the faithful can walk through darkness without fear of the shadow of death (cf. Matt 4:16; Job 29:3).

The task then of the new Israel in Jesus Christ is to proclaim the "wonderful deeds" of God; to so preach and teach and live as to announce to all people everywhere that they need no longer walk in darkness or fear to pass through the valley of death; that there is truth by which they may be guided and a mercy by which they may be forgiven and restored to fellowship with the one God "who abolished death and brought life and immortality to light through the gospel" (1 Tim 1:10). The new Israel in our Lord—the Christian church—is to shine forth in the world with that good news, as Israel's truth about God was to illumine its world.

The text of Zech 4:1–14 tells us how we can do that—how we can be modern-day evangels of God's gospel. We can

180

be a light to the world only as we ourselves are fueled, fed, inspired by the Spirit of God. On our own we have no light to illumine the darkness of humankind. By our own strong commitment and plentiful resources we cannot communicate the good news to any. Our programs may be many, our wealth put at our service, our planning and advertising and curricula aimed at evangelizing the world. Our teaching and preaching may be expert and moving and sometimes even brilliant, but unless we speak out of the Spirit of God, we will make no true disciples. Our light comes from God's light through the Spirit of Jesus Christ, and apart from the Spirit, it is darkness.

But how do we find and receive the Spirit of God? There is lots of talk these days about "having the Spirit," and much of it is bogus. We can even be led astray by false spirits who have nothing to do with the Holy Spirit. It is not for nothing that 1 John warns us, "Test the spirits to see whether they are of God; for many false prophets have gone out into the world" (4:1). We need to know how we may ascertain if we have received the Holy Spirit.

Our text furnishes us with the answer. In its symbolism it tells us that the Spirit of God is given to the people of God through those two mediators, the high priest and the Davidic Messiah. The one true Spirit comes only through them. And in the New Testament, our Lord Jesus Christ has become both our high priest (Heb 4:14–16) and our Davidic Messiah-King (Matt 21:9; John 20:31, et al.). Jesus Christ is the mediator to us of the Spirit of God, continuing his work among us by means of the Spirit (cf. John 14:25–26; 16:7; Rom 8:11; 2 Cor 3:17–18, etc.). God has poured his Spirit into our hearts (cf. Rom 5:5), and that Spirit is Jesus Christ (2 Cor 3:17). Only as the Spirit speaks and acts in accordance with Christ, as the Scriptures witness to him, is he the true Spirit of God.

In short, we can be a light to the world only as we live in Christ—only as we know him through the Scriptures and seek him daily in prayer, only as we cleave to his commands and depend on his mercy for our lives, only as we teach and preach him to the world and make him the center of our church life.

We have been given, in the Christian church, the means of receiving Christ's Spirit through those things that are termed "the means of grace." By that phrase is meant primarily the preaching, reading, and teaching of the Word of God in the Bible, and the sacraments of baptism and Lord's Supper. Through them especially, Christ's Spirit is given to us. But we might also say that Christ's Spirit comes to us through the worship of the congregation, the fellowship of believers, and the daily practice of obedience. By all of those gracious means Christ lends his Spirit to us. And by participation in them, we participate in our Lord. To receive the Spirit of Jesus Christ, therefore, we should continually and consistently seek after these avenues of his grace.

Jesus told us once that "apart from me you can do nothing," (John 15:5). And that means that no activity or message of the church can contribute to the purpose of God apart from Jesus Christ. It is a message similar to that which Zechariah gave us. "Not by might, nor by power, but by my Spirit, says the LORD of hosts."

Index of Correlations
to the Common Lectionary

Index of Scripture References

3:13 86
4:14 91
4:16 88
6:1–2 86
6:6 88
7:1–6 86–91
7:9–10 86–91
8:6 88
8:10 86
9:2 91
9:20–22 86–91
9:26–28 87

Job
1–2 96
1:21 97
1:22 97
2:1 95
2:1–10 95–100
2:4 97
2:9 97
2:10 98
9:5 164
9:7 164
9:11 99
9:34 99
13:3 99
13:20–24 99
19:25–27 100
23:3 99
29 96
29:1–4 99
29:3 180
30:20 99
31:35 99
38–41 100
38:8–10 135
38:8–11 133
38:31–33 164
42:1–9 100

Psalms
5:10 109
8:5 149
10:2 109
17:14 109
18:34 27
18:39 27
18:48 27
20:5–9 27

21:8–13 27
25:8 6
27:1 180
28:4 109
29:3–9 33
29:6 102
29:10 135
34:8 6
34:15–16 3
35 25
40:6–8 51
43:3 180
44:23 132
45:4–5 27
46 106, 135
46:1–3 134
46:5 107
46:6 33
48 106
48:3 107
48:8 107
51:16–17 51
66:10 20
73 155
73:25–26 100
74:13–14 134
76 106
76:12 108
78:65 132
79:1 143
79:4 143
79:10 108, 143
81:7 20
84 106
84:11 107
85:10–11 3
86:15 5
87 106
89:9–10 134
89:22–23 27
96:8 39
96:9 102
97:1–5 33
97:2 40
97:3 40
97:4 40
97:5 40
99:1 102, 104
100:3 149
103:2–5 98–99

103:8 5
103:14 5
104:4 33
104:5–9 33, 133
104:20–21 164
104:29–30 164
104:32 33
105 128
110:1 27
110:5–6 27
114 101–4
114:1 101
114:2 102
114:3–4 102
114:7 102, 104
114:8 102
115:1–2 143
119:130 180
122 106
124 86
132:18 27
137 105–10
137:1–3 105
137:1–6 105
137:1–7 110
137:4 105
137:4–6 105
137:4–7 109, 110
137:5–7 108
137:7 107, 109
137:7–9 105
137:8 107
137:8–9 109, 110
137:9 105, 107
139:2 176
144:1 27
144:5 33
145:8 5
147:15–18 164

Proverbs
1–9 112
1:20 112
1:33 112
2:9 112
6:22 112
7:4 112
8:1 112
8:1–4 111–15
8:4–5 112

188

Index of Scripture References

190

1:8–9   174
1:12   98, 174–75
1:14–18   xiv, 173–77
1:15   173
1:18   174
2:1   177
2:3   177
3:9–13   175
3:14–17   175

Zechariah
1:7–2:13   179
3:1–6:15   179
4:1   179
4:1–14   178–82
4:6   178, 179, 182
4:6–7   179
4:7–10   179
4:8–10   179
4:10–14   179
4:11   179
4:12   179

Malachi
1:6   26
2:10   26
2:10–16   80
2:16   82, 119
3:17   97

NEW TESTAMENT

Matthew
1:1   90
2:14   153
3:2   171
3:15   42
4:16   180
5–7   35
5:4   145
5:14   180
5:16   140
5:44   91
5:45   165
5:48   168
6:22   179
6:26   164
6:28–30   164
7:21   35, 176

8:11   55
8:20   153
9:13   51, 65
9:16–17   6
10:29   164
10:30   176
10:32   176
10:34   27
10:37   67
11:4–5   124–25
11:19   153
12:7   51, 65
14:17   33
16:24   35
17:2   38
19:28   154
21:9   181
24   173, 176–77
25   173
25:21   155
25:23   155
25:31–46   176
26:39   22
27:46   22
27:51–52   164
28:2   103
28:6   103

Mark
1:15   54, 124, 171
2:12   153
4:35–41   134
5:25–34   32
7:21   119, 159
8:31   153
8:38   153
9:2–8   76
9:9   153
9:11   153
9:37   176
9:38–50   86
10:9–10   82
10:17–20   35
10:17–21   42
10:21   66
10:33   153
11:17   4
12:20   176
12:28–31   42
12:30   90, 140, 150

12:33   65
13:7   55
13:26   153
13:35   177
14:62   153
15:29–32   108

Luke
2:9   39, 41
2:10   33
5:8   73
6:20–31   153
6:22–23   154
8:46   71
9:29   38
9:62   67
11:20   54, 171
12:32   73
17:21   171
18:1   170
18:13   131, 177
23:34   54, 110, 170
23:44–45   164
24:31   108

John
1:4   180
1:9   180
1:21   54
1:25   54
1:29   7
3:14–15   44
4:10–15   104
4:14   104
5:17   176
6:6   20
6:14   54
7:40   54
9:3   166
10:10   129
12:28–30   33
14:6   35
14:25–26   181
15:1   153
15:5   182
16:7   181
16:12–15   111
18:33–19:22   29
20:31   181

Acts
3:22–26 54
7:37 54
7:52 54
26:18 154

Romans
1:16 21
1:24–31 171
3:25 5
5:1–5 111
5:5 181
5:8 15, 25, 61
6:1–4 7
8:11 181
8:17 154
8:21 42
8:26–27 170
8:28 129
8:31 4
8:34 54, 170
8:39 30
11 90
11:17–24 90
12:19 109
16:1–3 15
16:3 15

1 Corinthians
1:12 154
1:30 111, 114
6:9 119
6:9–11 159
7:12–14 84
10:16 55
11:4–16 16
13:12 54, 100
14:33–35 16
14:33–36 16
14:36 16
15:25 27

2 Corinthians
1:22 55
3:6 41
3:7–18 38, 41
3:13 41
3:14–16 42
3:17 42, 181
3:17–18 181
3:18 43

4:6 38, 42, 43
5:5 55
5:10 176
6 84
6:14 84
6:15 84
8:2 20
12:21 119

Galatians
3:28 15, 120
4:3–7 26
5:19 119
6:7 176
6:16 xi, 90

Ephesians
1:10 172
1:11–23 153
1:18 154
2:11–18 90
5 15
5:5 119
5:21 16, 120
5:21–33 16
6:12 29
6:13 29
6:18 171

Philippians
2:11 172

Colossians
3:5 119

1 Thessalonians
4:3–8 119
5:17 171

1 Timothy
1:10 119, 180
1:3–7 16
2:9 16
5:6 16
5:13–16 16

2 Timothy
2:11–12 154
3:1–9 16
4:3–4 16

Titus
2:3–5 16
3:9 16

Hebrews
3:1 33
3:8 20
4:14–16 74, 181
4:15 168
10:30 109
11:17 20
12:18–24 34
12:22–24 36
12:28–29 37
13:4 119

James
1:2–3 20
5:13–20 86
5:16 171

1 Peter
2:9 180
2:9–10 90
2:10 26

1 John
4:1 181
4:19 99

Revelation
1:17 73
21:1–2 136
21:3–4 136

APOCRYPHA

Wisdom
7:24 112
7:27 112
7:30 112

Ecclesiasticus
24:23 114
24:32 114
24:33 114